AAT

TUTORIAL TEXT

CW00321409

Intermediate Units 4 and 5

Financial Accounting

August 1997 edition

The fifth edition of this Tutorial Text has the following improvements.

- Full account is taken of recent Central Assessments.

- Material on leases and SSAP 21 has been added as a result of information from the AAT.

- Feedback on the last edition, from both students and lecturers, has been taken into account.

FOR JUNE 1998 AND DECEMBER 1988 ASSESSMENTS

First edition 1993
Fifth edition August 1997

ISBN 0 7517 6083 8 (previous edition 0 7517 6063 3)

British Library Cataloguing-in-Publication Data

A catalogue record for this book
is available from the British Library

Published by

BPP Publishing Limited
Aldine House, Aldine Place
London W12 8AW

We are grateful to the Lead Body for Accounting for permission to reproduce extracts from the Standards of Competence for Accounting.

Printed by Ashford Colour Press, Gosport, Hants

HOW TO USE THIS TUTORIAL TEXT

This Tutorial Text covers Unit 4: *Recording capital transactions* and Unit 5: *Preparing financial accounts*. It is designed to be used alongside BPP's Units 4 and 5 *Financial Accounting* Workbook, which provides Practice Exercises on the material covered in this Tutorial Text, together with Devolved Assessments and Central Assessments.

As you complete each chapter of this Tutorial Text, work through the *Practice Exercises* in the corresponding section of the Workbook. Once you have completed all of the Sessions of Practice Exercises, you will be in a position to attempt the Devolved and Central Assessments.

The tasks involved in a *Devolved Assessment* will vary in length and complexity, and there may be more than one 'scenario'. If you complete all of the Devolved Assessments in the Workbook, you will have gained practice in all parts of the elements of competence included in Units 4 and 5. You can then test your competence by attempting the Trial Run Devolved Assessment, which is modelled on the type of assessment actually set by the AAT.

Of course you will also want to practise the kinds of task which are set in the *Central Assessments*. The main Central Assessment section of the BPP Workbook includes all the AAT Central Assessments set from December 1993 to December 1994, and by doing them you will get a good idea of what you will face in the assessment hall. When you feel you have mastered all relevant skills, you can attempt the five Trial Run Central Assessments in the Workbook. These consist of the June 1995 to June 1997 Central Assessments. Provided you are competent, they should contain no unpleasant surprises, and you should feel confident of performing well in your actual Central Assessment.

A note on pronouns

For reasons of style, it is sometimes necessary in our study material to use 'he' instead of 'he or she', 'him' instead of 'him or her' and so on. However, no prejudice or stereotyping according to sex is intended or assumed.

Introduction

STANDARDS OF COMPETENCE

The competence-based Education and Training Scheme of the Association of Accounting Technicians (AAT) is based on an analysis of the work of accounting staff in a wide range of industries and types of organisation. The Standards of Competence for Accounting which students are expected to meet are based on this analysis.

The Standards identify the *key purpose* of the accounting occupation, which is to operate, maintain and improve systems to record, plan, monitor and report on the financial activities of an organisation, and a number of *key roles* of the occupation. Each key role is subdivided into *units of competence*. By successfully completing assessments in specified units of competence, students can gain qualifications at NVQ/SVQ levels 2, 3 and 4, which correspond to the AAT Foundation, Intermediate and Technician stages of competence respectively.

Intermediate stage key roles and units of competence

The key roles and unit titles for the AAT Intermediate stage (NVQ/SVQ level 3) are set out below.

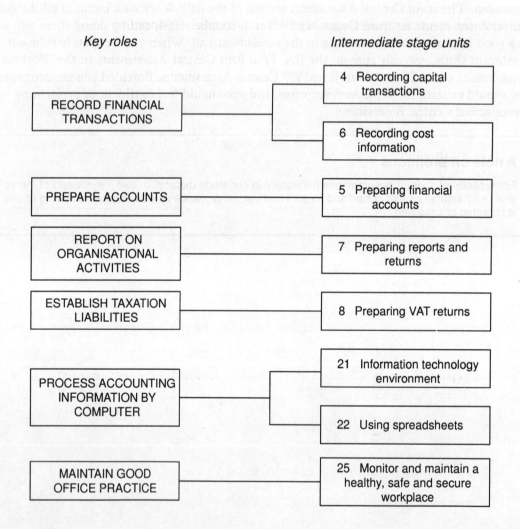

Units and elements of competence

Units of competence are divided into *elements of competence* describing activities which the individual should be able to perform.

Each element includes a set of *performance criteria* which define what constitutes competent performance. Each element also includes a *range statement* which defines the situations, contexts, methods etc in which the competence should be displayed.

Supplementing the standards of competence are statements of *knowledge and understanding* which underpin competent performance of the standards.

The elements of competence for Unit 4: *Recording capital transactions* and Unit 5: *Preparing financial accounts* are set out below. For each unit, the performance criteria are listed first, followed by the knowledge and understanding required for the unit as a whole. These are cross-referenced to chapters in this BPP Tutorial Text, which correspond with sessions of exercises in the corresponding Workbook.

Unit 4: Recording capital transactions

4.1 Maintain records and accounts relating to capital expenditure

Performance criteria		Chapter(s) in this Text
1	Relevant details relating to specific items of capital expenditure are correctly entered in the appropriate records	4
2	The organisation's records agree with the physical presence of capital items	4
3	Any acquisition and disposal costs and revenues are correctly identified and recorded	4
4	Depreciation charges and other necessary entries and adjustments are correctly calculated and recorded in the appropriate ledger accounts	4
5	Where required, the records show clearly the prior authority for capital expenditure and indicate the approved method of funding	4
6	The organisation's policies, regulations, procedures and timescales are observed	4
7	Discrepancies, unusual features or queries are identified and either resolved or referred to the appropriate person	4

Range statement

1   Entries relating to tax allowances are excluded

2   Depreciation methods: straight line, reducing balance

3   Discrepancies, unusual features or queries include lack of agreement between physical items and records

Introduction

Knowledge and understanding

The business environment

Chapter(s)
in this Text

- Types and characteristics of different types of asset — 4
- Main requirements of SSAP 12 or any relevant FRS — 4
- Relevant legislation and regulations (public sector organisations) — 4

Accounting techniques

- Methods of depreciation — 4

- Accounting treatment of capital items sold, scrapped or otherwise retired from service — 4

- Use of plant registers and similar subsidiary records — 4

- Use of transfer journal — 1

Accounting principles and theory

- Basic accounting concepts and principles: matching of income and expenditure within an accounting period, historic cost, accruals, consistency, prudence, materiality — 2

- Principles of double entry accounting — 1

- Distinction between capital and revenue expenditure, what constitutes capital expenditure — 4

The organisation

- Background understanding that the system of an organisation are affected by its organisational structure, its administrative systems and procedures and the nature of its business transactions — 4

Unit 5: Preparing financial accounts

5.1 Record income and expenditure

	Performance criteria	Chapter(s) in this text
1	Income and expenditure is correctly recorded in the appropriate ledger accounts	5, 9
2	Any accrued or prepaid income and expenditure is correctly identified and adjustments are made	6, 9
3	The organisation's policies, regulations, procedures and timescales are observed	5, 6, 9
4	Income and expenditure is analysed in accordance with defined requirements and appropriate information is passed to management	5, 6, 9
5	Discrepancies, unusual features or queries are identified and either resolved or referred to the appropriate person	5, 9

Range statement

1   Items of income and expenditure for an organisation, including capital receipts and payments

5.2 Prepare accounts from incomplete records

	Performance criteria	Chapter(s) in this Text
1	Essential accounts and reconciliations are correctly prepared	8
2	Existing primary information is accurately summarised	7, 9
3	Other relevant information is correctly identified and recorded	7, 9
4	Investigations into the client's business transactions are conducted with tact and courtesy	6
5	The organisation's policies, regulations, procedures and timescales are observed	7, 8, 9
6	Discrepancies, unusual features or queries are identified and either resolved or referred to the appropriate person	7, 8, 9

Range statement

1   Reconstructing any accounts from data in an unusual or incomplete form

2   Discrepancies, unusual features or queries include situations where insufficient data has been provided, where there are inconsistencies within the data

5.3 Prepare the extended trial balance

	Performance criteria	Chapter(s) in this text
1	The trial balance is accurately extended and totalled	10
2	Totals from the general ledger or other records are correctly entered on the extended trial balance	10
3	Any errors disclosed by the trial balance are traced and corrected	10
4	Any adjustments not dealt with in the ledger accounts are correctly entered on the extended trial balance	10
5	An agreed valuation of closing stock is correctly entered on the extended trial balance	10
6	The organisation's policies, regulations, procedures and timescales are observed	10
7	Discrepancies, unusual features or queries are identified and either resolved or referred to the appropriate person	10

Range statement

Relevant accounting policies include the treatment of depreciation and other provisions

Unit 5: Knowledge and understanding

The column headed *Elements* indicates the elements of Unit 5 under which the area of knowledge and understanding is listed in the Standards of Competence.

The business environment	Elements	Chapter(s) in this Text
• General function and status of SSAPs and FRSs	5.1, 5.2, 5.3	3
• Main requirements of SSAPs 2, 5, 9, 12, 13 and 21 as they affect this element and any relevant FRSs	5.2, 5.3	3 - 7
• Legal, VAT and tax requirements	5.2	3, 5
• Need to present accounts in the correct form	5.2	3, 6
Accounting techniques		
• Accounting treatment of accruals and prepayments	5.1, 5.2, 5.3	6, 9
• Use of transfer journal	5.1, 5.2, 5.3	5
• Methods of analysing income and expenditure	5.1	5, 9
• Methods of restructuring accounts from incomplete evidence	5.2	8
• Correction of different types of error	5.2, 5.3	8, 9, 10
• Making and adjusting provisions	5.2, 5.3	8, 9, 10
Accounting principles and theory		
• Principles of double entry accounting	5.1, 5.3	1
• Basic accounting concepts and principles - matching of income and expenditure within an accounting period, historic cost, accruals, consistency, prudence, materiality	5.1	2
• Function and form of accounts for income and expenditure	5.1	5
• Function and form of a trial balance	5.2, 5.3	1, 7, 8
• Basic principles of stock valuation: cost or NRV; what is included in cost	5.2, 5.3	7
• Objectives of making provisions for depreciation and other purposes	5.2, 5.3	4
The organisation		
• Background understanding that the system of an organisation is affected by its organisational structure, its administrative systems and procedures and the nature of its business transactions	5.1, 5.2, 5.3	5

ASSESSMENT STRUCTURE

Devolved and central assessment

The units of competence at the Intermediate stage are assessed by a combination of devolved assessment and central assessment.

Devolved assessment tests students' ability to apply the skills detailed in the relevant units of competence. Devolved assessment may be carried out by means of:

(a) simulations of workplace activities set by AAT-approved assessors; or
(b) observation in the workplace by AAT-approved assessors.

Central assessments are set and marked by the AAT, and concentrate on testing students' grasp of the knowledge and understanding which underpins units of competence.

The Intermediate Stage

Units of competence at the AAT Intermediate stage (NVQ/SVQ level 3) are tested by central assessment (CA) and devolved assessment (DA) as follows.

Unit number		Central assessment	Devolved assessment
4	Recording capital transactions		✓
5	Preparing financial accounts	✓	✓
6	Recording cost information	✓	✓
7	Preparing reports and returns	✓	✓
8	Preparing VAT returns		✓
21	Information technology environment		✓
22	Using spreadsheets		✓
25*	Monitor and maintain a healthy, safe and secure workplace		✓

Note. If you have covered Unit 25 Health, Safety and Security at Foundation level, you do not need to study it again. If not, a *Health and Safety at Work* booklet may be obtained from BPP (see order form at the end of this Tutorial Text).

Central Assessment (FA): Preparing Financial Accounts

The Central Assessment *Preparing Financial Accounts* covers underpinning knowledge and understanding for Unit 5 and can be expected to be divided into sections as follows.

Section 1   Extended trial balance exercise
Section 2   Short answer questions with some communication tasks
Section 3   Incomplete records exercise

All questions and tasks in all parts are to be attempted: none is optional. The total time allowed is three hours.

The main topics to be assessed are: relevant accounting concepts and principles, the nature and classification of assets and liabilities, capital and revenue expenditure, objectives and principles of depreciation, and relevant accounting standards.

Introduction

FURTHER GUIDANCE

In his *Assessment manual* the AAT has produced the following guidance on the assessments for Units 4 and 5.

Central assessment: *Financial Accounting*

Part 1

Part 1 is an accounting exercise which gives a brief description of the business and a list of period-end accounts balances. A fair sample of the main types of account will be included although the scale of the tasks will not be as great as would be expected in a devolved assessment. Candidates will be required to prepare an extended trial balance and deal with adjustments such as accruals and prepayments, depreciation, provisions etc. Error corrections and other adjustments, possibly requiring journal entries, may also be a part of the exercise.

Part 2

This consists of a number of short-answer questions to test communication skills, knowledge and understanding. These may require brief explanations, calculations, accounting entries, selection from a number of given possible answers, or other similar responses. Some of the responses will be in the form of memos and/or draft letters. Examples of aspects which could be included are:

Depreciation
Stock valuation
Other year end adjustments
Function of trial balance
Accounting concepts and principles
Accounting standards (general function and effects)
Capital and revenue distinction
VAT regulations and entries

Part 3

There will be one or more practical accounting problems in non-standard form involving the processing or re-structuring of given data to produce the information required. This is to test the candidates' understanding of the inter-relationships within the data and the ability to handle less routine situations. Incomplete records problems are a strong possibility for inclusion but additionally or alternatively there could be problems involving aspects such as stock valuation, fixed asset transactions and depreciation, accruals and prepayments etc.

Devolved assessment

General principles

All students should collect evidence of competence in the relevant units at the Intermediate Stage and present this for assessment in the form of a portfolio of work. The portfolio might include evidence obtained from the workplace, simulations and projects undertaken at college or the workplace.

Specific guidance for each unit

The following examples are designed to suggest the types of evidence that students might collect for their portfolio at the Intermediate Stage. The list is not exhaustive, and assessors and mentors should use their own judgement in deciding on the relevance of a particular piece of evidence.

Recording capital transactions

Few students are likely to maintain capital records as part of their work experience. Most evidence will therefore be likely to be in the form of simulations. The portfolio should include at least one example of each of the exercises below.

Possible simulations:

(a) Record the purchase, sale and depreciation of assets in realistically designed asset registers (eg vehicle, plant registers)

(b) Exercise/case which includes dealing with a discrepancy between physical items and the records

(c) Problems on the straight line and reducing balance methods of depreciation

Preparing financial accounts

Workplace evidence can be presented, where possible, but it is unlikely that it will cover all aspects of the Standards except in the case of a small firm. The main object is to ensure that accounting exercises are realistic and include a sufficient number of contingencies. They should be competence-based rather than mechanical text book exercises. The portfolio should include a wide spread of relevant simulations (eg at least one of each type of exercise listed below), including a number which are computer-based.

Possible simulations:

(a) Incomplete records (a common form of simulated exercise, many good examples available)
(b) Long accounting exercises with accruals, pre-payments etc
(c) Trial balance with adjustments
(d) Correction of error exercises
(e) Exercises showing the analysis of income and expenditure

BPP MEETS THE AAT

On behalf of students, BPP keeps in touch with the AAT and seeks to determine the approach which should be followed in an assessment. On this page, we summarise the points in question and answer form.

What is the correct treatment for drawings of business stock for personal use?

The traditional view is:

DEBIT   Drawings
CREDIT   Purchases

at cost price.

However, the AAT's recommended treatment, according better with modern practice and the requirements of HM Customs & Excise, is as follows.

DEBIT   Drawings at selling price (including VAT)
CREDIT   Sales
CREDIT   VAT

In the March 1995 edition of the Education and Training Newsletter, acknowledging the variation in practice and between different VAT offices, the AAT stated that the traditional method would be accepted, but you should try to use the newer, recommended method if information on VAT is available.

Are manufacturing accounts assessed at the Intermediate Stage?

Yes, but only the basic principles. For example, as part of an incomplete records exercise manufacturing accounts could be assessed, but only to draw up a P&L account, *not* full-blown accounts. Students should know the principles. This approach is justified by the range statement under 5.2 which could cover *any account*.

The principles involved could be assessed, eg calculation of cost of stock, but there will be NO assessment of the 'fringe' areas.

Could club accounts be assessed?

Yes, club accounts could feature as part of an incomplete records question.

Are hire purchase transactions assessable (SSAP 21)?

Yes, this is explicitly mentioned in the Standards of Competence (elements 5.2 and 5.3), but only very basic aspects would be tested, eg treatment, what might appear in financial accounts, not 'T' accounts. An example of the type of question set is task 2.3 from the December 1996 Central Assessment.

Is it correct that only a background knowledge of the nature of partnerships and companies is requires?

You are right in your understanding that a background knowledge of the nature of partnerships and companies is required and that the detailed accounting aspects are not assessable until Technician Stage. If company extended trial balances are covered, clear guidance will be given to candidates and additional accounts (ie beyond share capital and profit and loss accounts) will not be included.

Part A
The framework of accounting

2

1 Double entry bookkeeping: revision

This chapter covers the following topics.

1   **Introduction**

2   **Posting from primary records to ledger accounts**

3   **The interrelationship between accounts: double entry**

4   **More about double entry**

5   **The financial statements**

6   **Using the journal**

7   **Bad and doubtful debts**

8   **From ledgers to financial statements: an overview**

9   **From ledgers to financial statements: the mechanics**

1   INTRODUCTION

1.1   If you have successfully completed your studies at the AAT Foundation stage, you will by now have a good grasp of the principles of double entry bookkeeping. Your Foundation studies have covered cash, credit and payroll transactions and the related documentation and double entry.

1.2   The purpose of this chapter is to refresh the memory of those of you who have taken the Foundation stage (NVQ/SVQ level 2) and to provide a brief introduction to double entry bookkeeping for those of you who have not. This may also act as revision if you have studied bookkeeping or accounting elsewhere. You are advised to read through this chapter and make sure that you are happy with its contents, before going on with the rest of the text.

1.3   An organisation's transactions are recorded by the accounting system, so that *reports* can be made to management. The diagram below summarises this process.

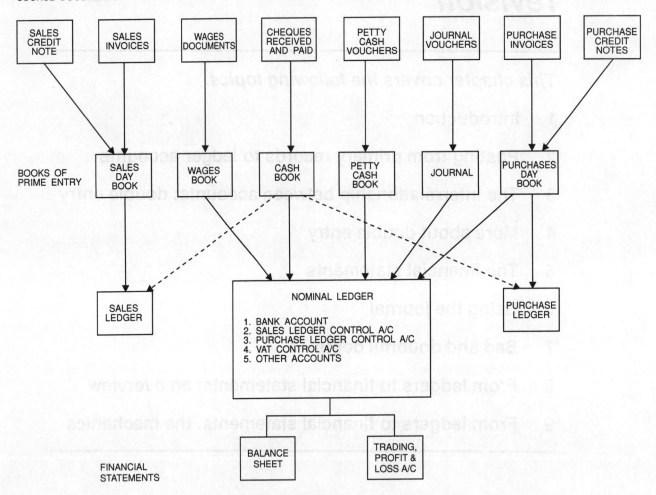

2   POSTING FROM PRIMARY RECORDS TO LEDGER ACCOUNTS

Source documents

2.1   The reason why source documents are given this name is because they are the source of all the information recorded by a business. Here are some examples.

(a) Petty cash vouchers
(b) Cheques received
(c) Cheque stubs (for cheques paid out)
(d) Stock records
(e) Wages, salary and PAYE records
(f) VAT returns

(g) Sales invoices
(h) Purchase invoices

Recording of source documents

2.2 During the course of its business, an organisation sends out and receives many source documents. The details on these source documents need to be *summarised*, as otherwise the business might forget to ask for some money, or forget to pay some, or even accidentally pay something twice. In other words, it needs to keep records of source documents - of transactions - so that it can keep tabs on what is going on.

2.3 Such records are made in *books of prime entry*. The main books of prime entry are as follows.

(a) The *sales day book*. This lists all invoices sent to debtors (ie customers). Each invoice will have a number, as the sales day book is in sequence. It will be totalled (added up) at the end of each day.

(b) The *purchases day book*. This lists all invoices received from creditors (ie suppliers). Again, these are written down when received and added up at the end of each day.

(c) The *cash book*. This is also a day book, which is used to keep a record of money received and money paid out by the businesses, with a running total of money held (or owed on an overdraft).

(d) The *petty cash book*. Most businesses keep a small amount of cash on the premises to make occasional small payments in cash, eg to pay the milkman, to buy a few postage stamps or pay the office cleaner.

(e) The *journal*. This records alterations to nominal ledger accounts. The journal is described below.

2.4 These books of prime entry are then used to 'post' items to *ledger accounts*.

2.5 A ledger account is simply a list of transactions of a particular type. It can take almost any format, but it generally ensures that records are:

(a) in *chronological order*, and *dated* so that transactions can be related to a particular period of time; and

(b) built up in *cumulative totals*, eg:

(i) day by day (eg total sales on Monday, total sales on Tuesday);
(ii) week by week;
(iii) month by month;
(iv) year by year.

2.6 Here is an example.

ADVERTISING EXPENSES

Date	Narrative	Folio	£	Date	Narrative	Folio	£
19X6				19X6			
3.1	JFK Agency for	PL48	2,500	13.1	Refund from JFK	PR271	125
12.1	Ruby, Oswald	PL274	1,500				
21.1	CIA Agency	PL399	1,750				
23.1	KGB Advertising	PL420	1,000				
28.1	PCQ Media		1,800	31.1	Carried down		8,425
			8,550				8,550
1.2	Brought down		8,425				

What does this show?

(a) Every time we receive an invoice for advertising expenditure it is noted down here (and in another account too, to complete the double entry).

(b) There are actually two different kinds of transaction shown here. While we have 'incurred' (ie paid or agreed to pay) £8,550 of advertising expenditure in January, we have also received a refund of £125, so we have actually spent £8,550 – £125 = £8,425.

At the end of every month, or whatever period, we total up the account, so we know how much we've spent at the end of one period and the beginning of the next.

Main types of ledger account

The nominal ledger

2.7 As a business has many different types of expenditure (eg wages, advertising, purchases of raw materials), it will have many different types of *accounts* to contain them all.

Here are some examples of accounts.

(a) An account for the business's cars
(b) An account for wages
(c) An account to record sales revenue received or owing for a period
(d) Rent paid

2.8 Most ledger accounts are maintained in the *nominal ledger* (or *general ledger*). This is an accounting record which summarises the financial affairs of a business. It consists of a large number of different accounts, each having its own purpose or 'name' and an identity or code.

2.9 A ledger used to be a large book, and each page would be an account. Nowadays ledgers are often held on computer.

The sales ledger and purchase ledger

2.10 The *sales* (or *debtors*) *ledger* consists of a number of personal accounts, one for each customer who buys goods on credit. When a credit customer makes a purchase, the invoice is recorded in the *sales day book*. The invoice is then recorded using *the sales day book* in the customer's personal account in the sales ledger. When cash is received, it is recorded in the cash book and in the debtor's account in the sales ledger. In this way the business keeps a record of how much money it is owed who owes it.

2.11 The *purchase (or creditors) ledger*, like the sales ledger, consists of a number of personal accounts. These are separate accounts for each individual supplier, and they help a business to keep a continuous record of how much it owes each supplier at any time. Invoices (and other documents, such as credit notes) are recorded in the purchase ledger using the *purchases day book*. Cash paid to creditors is recorded in the cash book and in the creditor's account in the purchase ledger.

Control accounts

2.12 A control account is an account in the *nominal ledger* in which a record is kept of the *total value* of a number of similar but individual items.

(a) A *debtors control account* is an account in which records are kept of transactions involving all debtors in total. It is posted with totals from the *sales day book* and the *cash book*. The balance on the debtors control account at any time will be the total amount due to the business at that time from its debtors. This means that the total should equal the total of all the personal account balances in the sales ledger.

(b) A *creditors control account* is an account in which records are kept of transactions involving all creditors in total, being posted with totals from the purchases day book and the cash book. The balance on this account at any time will be the total amount owed by the business at that time to its creditors. The total should therefore equal the total of the list of individual balances in the purchases ledger.

(c) Control accounts can also be kept for other items, such as:

(i) stocks of goods; and

(ii) wages and salaries.

Remember, then, that a control account is an account which keeps a total record for a collective item (such as debtors) which in reality consists of many individual items (individual debtors). You can see then that a control account can be used as a *check* that the sum of the individual balances on the ledger is correct.

2.13 At the end of an *accounting period* (which might be a month, a quarter or a year) the accounts in the nominal ledger are used to produce *financial statements*. The accounts will (usually) be adjusted first for various reasons to produce the statements which consist of:

(a) the balance sheet; and

(b) the profit and loss account.

3 THE INTERRELATIONSHIP BETWEEN ACCOUNTS: DOUBLE ENTRY
Centrally assessed 6/94 - 6/97

3.1 The 'double entry' system of bookkeeping was first introduced in Venice in 1494 AD and it is known as the 'double entry' system because *each transaction is recorded twice*. This may seem strange, but it is based on a fundamental concept in accounting, that all the *assets* of a business are equal to the total of its *liabilities*. Assets are things that a business owns, like stock, and debts owed to the business. Liabilities are the debts the business owes to other people or businesses, and to the owners of the business. This last, special kind of liability is called *capital*7

The basic rule

3.2 The basic rule is: *every* financial transaction gives rise to *two* accounting entries of the same amount, one a *debit* and the other a *credit*. Debits and credits are best demonstrated by showing you an account from the records of a company.

NAME OF ACCOUNT

DEBIT SIDE	£	CREDIT SIDE	£

3.3 This is usually called a 'T' account but it will be shown in most of the rest of the text without the vertical and horizontal lines of the 'T'. This account is empty now but we will look at how transactions are entered into the account soon. We have already looked at one of these: advertising expenditure in Paragraph 2.6

3.4 What are debits and credits? When looking at any financial transaction, the following rules determine how it should be treated.

(a) An increase in an *expense* (eg a purchase of stationery) or an increase in an *asset* (eg a purchase of office furniture) is a *debit*.

(b) An increase in *income* (eg a sale) or an increase in a *liability* (eg buying on credit) is a *credit*.

(c) A decrease in an *asset* (eg paying out cash) is a *credit*.

(d) A decrease in a *liability* (eg settling a creditor's account) is a *debit*.

If you remember these rules then you should be able to identify which part of a transaction is a debit or a credit with little difficulty. Do not worry yet about how to decide which items are income, expenses, assets or liabilities. This will become clearer later on in your studies.

3.5 To make things a little bit clearer now, let us look at some of the entries we might put into an account, eg the cash account.

3.6

CASH ACCOUNT

	£		£

Let us assume that, at the beginning of 12 August 19X5, we have nothing in the cash account. We will now look at how some transactions would be entered in the cash account and in other accounts in the books of the business.

Example: Double entry

3.7 Suppose that the following transactions take place on 12 August.

(a) A sale is made for £1,500 in cash
(b) An electricity bill is paid for £40 in cash
(c) New shelves are bought for £1,000 cash for the managing director's office
(d) A purchase is made for £65 in cash

3.8 Remember that cash is an *asset*.

(a) If we receive £1,500 in cash we have *increased* cash, an *asset*. An increase in an asset is a *debit*. We have also *increased* sales, which is *income*; an increase in income is a *credit*. This transaction can therefore be written as:

DEBIT	Cash account	£1,500	
CREDIT	Sales account		£1,500

You should see a certain amount of logic here: there should be two entries because two things are happening, a cash receipt *and* a sale.

(b) A *decrease* in cash (an *asset*) is a *credit*. An *increase* in an *expense*, electricity, is a *debit*.

DEBIT	Electricity account	£40	
CREDIT	Cash account		£40

(c) An *increase* in an *asset* (the shelves) is a *debit*. A *decrease* in an *asset* (cash) is a *credit*.

DEBIT	Shelves (asset) account	£1,000	
CREDIT	Cash account		£1,000

(d) An *increase* in an *expense* (purchases) is a *debit*. A *decrease* in an *asset* (cash) is a *credit*.

DEBIT	Purchases account	£65	
CREDIT	Cash account		£65

We can look at the accounts in the books of the business in 'T' account form.

CASH ACCOUNT

	£		£
Sales a/c	1,500	Electricity a/c	40
		Shelves a/c	1,000
		Purchases a/c	65

SALES ACCOUNT

	£		£
		Cash a/c	1,500

ELECTRICITY ACCOUNT

	£		£
Cash a/c	40		

SHELVES (ASSET) ACCOUNT

	£		£
Cash a/c	1,000		

PURCHASES

	£		£
Cash a/c	65		

3.9 The situation is different if a transaction takes place, such as a sale or a purchase, but the cash paid or received does not change hands immediately. When goods are purchased or sold *on credit*, it is necessary to use *debtors and creditors accounts* to record the transactions.

3.10 Using the sale and purchases in the example above, let us suppose that the sale and purchase took place on 12 August 19X5, but that no cash was sent or received until 31 August 19X5.

SALES ACCOUNT

	£				£
		19X5			
		12 August	Debtors a/c		1,500

DEBTORS ACCOUNT

		£			£
19X5			19X5		
12 August	Sales a/c	1,500	31 August	Cash a/c	1,500

PURCHASES ACCOUNT

		£		£
19X5			19X5	
12 August	Creditors a/c	65		

CREDITORS ACCOUNT

		£			£
19X5			19X5		
31 August	Cash a/c	65	12 August	Purchases a/c	65

CASH ACCOUNT

		£			£
19X5			19X5		
31 August	Debtors a/c	1,500	31 August	Creditors a/c	65

3.11 Can you see the end result of the transactions is exactly the same as before because the debits and credits on the debtors and creditors accounts cancel each other out? The amounts held in the remaining accounts are the same as though a cash sale and a cash purchase had taken place.

4 MORE ABOUT DOUBLE ENTRY
Centrally assessed 6/94 - 6/97

4.1 In the previous sections we looked at a few ledger accounts, and we mentioned that a ledger account contains a list of transactions built up over time. These can be used for the following purposes.

(a) To tell you how much something cost
(b) To tell you how much you owe someone
(c) To tell you how much someone owes you
(d) To tell you how much income you have received

4.2 Assume you have £100 and you wish to start in business. However, you wish, for your own convenience, that the business should be a *separate accounting entity* from yourself personally.

(a) So you 'give' the business £100. You open two bank accounts, one in the North and one in the South, and deposit £50 in each.

(b) You open up a ledger accounting system. What would you do first of all? You would want to record the fact in your *business's* accounts that you've just invested £100 in two bank accounts.

CAPITAL

DR		CR
	Cash - North	£50
	Cash - South	£50

This capital account is saying: the business owes £100 to the owner.

CASH: NORTH			CASH: SOUTH	
Capital	£50		Capital	£50

These cash accounts state what has happened to the £100 invested in the business.

Nominal ledger accounts

4.3 You then start trading. Here are the accounts in your nominal ledger for January. You will note that at the end of January we have *totalled the accounts* and *brought down the balances*.

CREDITORS: NORTH

	£		£
C/d 31/1	500	Purchases: North	500
		B/d 1/2	500

CREDITORS: SOUTH

	£		£
C/d 31/1	400	Purchases: South	400
		B/d 1/2	400

CASH: NORTH

	£		£
Opening balance 1/1	50	Wages: North	300
Sales: North	500	C/d 31/1	250
	550		550
B/d 1/2	250		

CASH: SOUTH

	£		£
Opening balance 1/1	50	Purchases: South	100
Sales: South	500	Wages: South	300
		C/d 31/1	150
	550		550
B/d 1/2	150		

CAPITAL

	£		£
		Opening balance 1/1	100

SALES: NORTH

	£		£
		Debtors: North (credit sales)	500
C/d 31/1	1,000	Cash: North (cash sales)	500
	1,000		1,000
		B/d 1/2	1,000

PURCHASES: NORTH

	£		£
Creditors: North (credit purchases)	500	C/d 3/1	500
B/d 1/2	500		

SALES: SOUTH

	£		£
		Debtors: South (credit sales)	700
C/d 31/1	1,200	Cash: South (cash sales)	500
	1,200		1,200

B/d 1/2   1,200

PURCHASES: SOUTH

	£		£
Creditors: South (credit purchases)	400		
Cash: South (cash purchases)	100	C/d 31/1	500
	500		500
B/d 1/2	500		

WAGES: NORTH

	£		£
Cash: North	300	C/d 31/1	300
B/d 1/2	300		

WAGES: SOUTH

	£		£
Cash: South	300	C/d 31/1	300
B/d 1/2	300		

DEBTORS: NORTH

	£		£
Sales: North	500	C/d	500
B/d	500		

DEBTORS: SOUTH

	£		£
Sales: South	700	C/d	700
B/d	700		

What information can be gleaned from these ledger accounts?

(a) How much has the whole business made in *profit*?

		Dr £	Cr £
Balance on South	Sales (revenue)		1,200
Balance on North	Sales (revenue)		1,000
Balance on South	Purchases (expense)	500	
Balance on North	Purchases (expense)	500	
Balance on South	Wages	300	
Balance on North	Wages	300	

The business has made £600 in profit (the amount by which the credits exceed the debits). As there are ledger accounts for each division you can *analyse* the profit into geographical areas to compare them.

	North £	South £	Total £
Sales revenue	1,000	1,200	2,200
Purchases expense	(500)	(500)	(1,000)
Wages	(300)	(300)	(600)
	200	400	600

We can thus measure the performance over time of the different divisions. A statement such as this is formally called a profit and loss account.

(b) What does the business *own*, and what does it *owe*? What are its assets and its liabilities?

	North £	South £	Total £
Cash	250	150	400
Debtors	500	700	1,200
	750	850	1,600
Creditors	500	400	900
Net assets (assets less liabilities)	250	450	700

(c) How can a business own more than it owes? Well, it doesn't. It owes £700 to you, the owner! How?

	£
You invested	100
You've made a profit of	600
	700

This will be the balance on your *capital account*.

CAPITAL ACCOUNT

	£		£
		Cash invested	100
C/d 31/1	700	Profits	600
	700		700

4.4 This leads us to some *equations*.

(a)
$$\text{Assets} - \text{Liabilities} = \text{Capital}$$

Assets	–	Liabilities	=	Capital
(eg cash,		(creditors)		(owner's
debtors)				investment)

(b) Profit = Revenue – Expenditure

We have also seen that profit is the increase in net assets over a period.

(i) At the beginning, your business had £100 in cash and it owed you £100.

(ii) At the end, it had net assets (assets less liabilities) of £700. The increase in net assets is:

	£
Net assets at the end of the period	700
Net assets at beginning of period	(100)
Increase in net assets (ie profit)	600

4.5 There will be occasions when there are other factors leading to an increase in net assets, eg the owner might contribute more capital.

4.6 We shall now examine a business's financial statements in more detail.

5 THE FINANCIAL STATEMENTS

5.1 Financial statements, or final accounts, are produced by a business for *several reasons*, the chief ones being the need to calculate taxation on profit and statutory requirements to prepare final accounts. If the business is a limited company then it must follow strict rules as to how the final accounts are prepared and presented. Unincorporated businesses or organisations (sole traders, partnerships, clubs and societies) can use any form they want.

The balance sheet

5.2 A balance sheet is a statement of the liabilities, capital and assets of a business at a given moment in time. It is like a '*snapshot*' *photograph*, since it captures on paper a still image, frozen at a single moment in time, of something which is dynamic and continually changing. The balance sheet will usually show the position on the date which is the end of the accounting period of the business; an *accounting period* is usually one year, but most businesses also prepare accounts every month.

5.3 This is an example of a balance sheet; we will discuss each of the items in turn. The balance sheet has been marked to show whether each item is a debit (Dr) or a credit (Cr).

JENNINGS
BALANCE SHEET AS AT 31 DECEMBER 19X1

	£	£
Fixed assets at net book value		
Freehold premises		50,000
Fixtures and fittings		8,000
Motor vehicles		9,000
		67,000 (Dr)
Current assets		
Stocks	16,000	
Debtors	500	
Cash	400	
	16,900 (Dr)	
Current liabilities		
Bank overdraft	2,000	
Creditors	1,800	
Taxation payable	3,500	
	7,300 (Cr)	
Net current assets		9,600 (Dr)
		76,600 (Dr)
Long-term liabilities		
Loan		(25,000) (Cr)
Net assets		51,600 (Dr)
Capital		
Capital as at 1 January 19X1		47,600
Profit for the year		8,000
		55,600 (Cr)
Less drawings		(4,000) (Dr)
Capital as at 31 December 19X1		51,600 (Cr)

5.4 We will look briefly at each part of the balance sheet.

(a) *Fixed assets* are assets bought for use within the business, rather than for selling to a customer. A fixed asset must be used by the business and it must have a 'life' in use by the business of more than one year.

(b) *Current assets* are either:

(i) items owned by the business with the intention of turning them into cash within one year; or

(ii) cash, including money in the bank, owned by the business.

(c) *Current liabilities* are debts of the business that must be paid within a year. This will normally include the bank overdraft as overdrafts are repayable on demand unless special terms are negotiated.

(d) *Long-term liabilities* are debts which are not payable until some time after one year from the accounting date.

The trading, profit and loss account

5.5 The trading, profit and loss account is a statement in which revenues (income) and expenditure are compared to arrive at a figure of *profit* or *loss*.

(a) The *gross profit* is the result of a comparison between the revenue from selling goods and the cost of purchasing or producing those goods (the trading account).

(b) The *net profit* is the result of deducting *overhead costs* and adding *sundry income* from the gross profit figure (the profit and loss account).

5.6 Here is an example of a trading, profit and loss account.

JENNINGS
TRADING, PROFIT AND LOSS ACCOUNT
FOR THE YEAR ENDING 31 DECEMBER 19X1

		£	£
Sales			139,300 (Cr)
Cost of sales			87,100 (Dr)
Gross profit	Trading a/c		52,200
Other income			2,000 (Cr)
			54,200
Selling and distribution expenses		14,700	
Administration expenses	Profit and loss a/c	14,800	
Finance expenses		16,700	
			46,200 (Dr)
Net profit (taken to the balance sheet)			8,000 (Cr)

5.7 Once again we will examine each part in turn.

(a) *Sales* represents the value of sales excluding value added tax.

(b) *Cost of sales* is the production or purchase cost of the goods sold.

(c) *Other income* will include dividends or interest on investments, profits on the sale of fixed assets and any other miscellaneous income which cannot be classified as sales.

(d) *Selling and distribution expenses* are expenses connected with the process of selling and delivering goods to customers. They include the salaries of sales staff, the cost of maintaining delivery vans and so on.

(e) *Administration expenses* are the expenses of the management and administration of the business. They include rent and rates, insurance, the salaries of directors, management and office staff, and so on.

(f) *Finance expenses* include interest on a loan and bank overdraft interest and charges.

6   USING THE JOURNAL
Centrally assessed 6/94 - 6/96

6.1 Earlier we mentioned the book of prime entry known as *the journal*. This is a good point at which to explain the journal in more detail.

6.2 The *journal* is used to provide a permanent record, with narrative, of *unusual movements* between accounts. Although it is a book of prime entry, and it is not a part of the double entry bookkeeping system itself, the journal:

(a) indicates *both* the debit entry *and* the credit entry in the ledger accounts; and

(b) it is then used to post the transactions to the ledger accounts as a debit and also a credit entry.

6.3 The types of transactions recorded in the journal are as follows.

(a) Transactions which *correct errors*. For example, if an incorrect posting has been made in the accounts, the correction of the error will be noted in the journal, from which the ledger accounts will then be corrected.

(b) Transactions *transferring* an amount from an account in the nominal ledger to the profit and loss account. When the trading, profit and loss account of a business is prepared, the transfers from various ledger accounts to the profit and loss account (itself a ledger account) are first of all noted in the journal.

(c) Transactions *transferring* amounts from a ledger account which has been used as a 'collecting station' for a certain item, eg drawings, which are then transferred to the capital account.

The format of journal entries

6.4 Whatever type of transaction is being recorded, the format of a journal entry is as follows.

Date		Folio/Ref	Debit £	Credit £
xx/xx/xx	Account to be debited		X	
	Account to be credited			X
	(Narrative to explain the transaction)			

Notes

(a) Remember that, in due course, the ledger accounts will be written up to include the transactions listed in the journal.

(b) A narrative explanation should accompany each journal entry. It is necessary, for audit and control, to indicate the purpose and authority of every transaction which is not first recorded in another book of prime entry.

(c) The 'folio' is the reference to the relevant place in the general ledger where the item is posted.

The correction of errors

6.5 A journal can only deal with errors which can be corrected by means of a *double entry* in the ledger accounts. When errors are made which break the rule of double entry, that debits and credits must be equal, the initial step in identifying and correcting the error is to open up a *suspense account* to restore equality between total debits and total credits. Errors leading to the creation of a suspense account are then corrected by making a record in the journal.

6.6 There are several common types of error.

(a) *Errors of transposition.* Suppose that a sale is recorded in the sales account as £6,843 instead of £6,483, but it has been correctly recorded in the total debtors account as £6,483. The error is the transposition of the 4 and the 8. The consequence is that total debits will not be equal to total credits, and the imbalance will first of all lead to the creation of a suspense account. A useful clue to a transposition error is that the imbalance will always be divisible by 9 (eg the above imbalance is £360).

(b) *Errors of omission.* Omission means failing to record a transaction at all, or making a debit or credit entry, but not the corresponding double entry.

   (i) If a business receives an invoice from a supplier for, say, £250, the transaction might be omitted from the books entirely. When the omission is eventually discovered, it will be logged in the journal.

DEBIT	Purchases	£250	
CREDIT	Creditors		£250

   A transaction previously omitted

   (ii) If a business receives an invoice from a supplier for, say, £300, the creditor's account might be credited, but the debit entry in the purchases account might be omitted. In this case, since total debits and total credits would not be equal as a result of the omission, the first step in the correction procedure would be to open up a suspense account (to take the omitted debit entry of £300).

(c) *Errors of principle.* An error of principle involves making a double entry in the belief that the transaction is being entered in the correct accounts, but subsequently finding out that the accounting entry breaks the 'rules' of an accounting principle.

Suppose that the owner of the business sometimes takes cash out of the till for his personal use and during a certain year these takings amount to £280. The bookkeeper states that he or she has reduced cash sales by £280 so that the cash book could be made to balance. This would be an error of principle, to be corrected in the journal by:

DEBIT	Owner's account	£280
CREDIT	Sales	£280

An error of principle, in which sales were reduced to compensate for cash drawings not accounted for

(d) *Errors of commission.* These are errors whereby the bookkeeper makes a mistake in carrying out his or her task of recording transactions in the accounts. These errors include the following.

   (i) Putting a debit entry or a credit entry in the wrong account, eg if telephone expenses of £540 are debited to the electricity expenses account, an error of commission has occurred. The correction should be journalised.

DEBIT	Telephone expenses	£540
CREDIT	Electricity expenses	£540

Correction of an error: telephone expenses wrongly charged to the electricity account

   (ii) Errors of adding up (casting) in the sales day book or purchase day book, eg the total day's credit sales in the sales day book of a business should add up to £28,425, but are incorrectly added up as £28,825. The total sales in the sales day book are then used to credit total sales and debit total debtors in the ledger accounts, so that total debits and total credits are still equal, although incorrect. The error, once identified, would be corrected after being logged in the journal.

DEBIT	Sales	£400
CREDIT	Debtors	£400

The correction of a casting error in the sales day book

Why is it necessary to journalise corrections of errors?

6.7 Errors which are corrected are logged in the journal because the journal provides a lasting *diary or record* of such mistakes, which might be of some value as information to management and could help in the prevention of fraud.

Journal vouchers

6.8 Journal entries might be logged, not in a single 'book' or journal, but on a separate slip of paper, called a *journal voucher*. A journal voucher is used to record the equivalent of one entry in the journal. Its fairly widespread use is perhaps explained by:

(a) the repetitive nature of certain journal entries. Vouchers can be pre-printed, to standardise the narrative of such entries, and to save time in writing them out;

(b) a voucher is able to hold more information than a conventional journal record.

7 BAD AND DOUBTFUL DEBTS
Centrally assessed 6/94 - 6/97

7.1 This subject was covered in your Foundation studies for Unit 2 *Credit Transactions* and is often tested at Intermediate level. Some businesses will not have bad debts, particularly retail operations, which do not sell goods on credit. If you don't have any debtors, you can't have any bad debts!

7.2 In the case of most wholesaling and manufacturing businesses and some service businesses there will be customers who buy goods on credit. For some older debts on the ledger, there may be little or no prospect of the business being paid, usually because the customer has gone bankrupt or is out of business. In some cases, dishonesty may be involved.

7.3   For one reason or another, therefore, a business might decide to give up expecting payment and to write the debt off as a 'lost cause'.

Bad debts written off: ledger accounting entries

7.4   For bad debts written off, there is a *bad debts account*. The double-entry bookkeeping is fairly straightforward, but there are two separate transactions to record.

(a)   When it is decided that a particular debt will not be paid, the customer is no longer called an outstanding debtor, and becomes a bad debt. We therefore:

DEBIT	Bad debts account (expense)
CREDIT	Debtors control account

(b)   At the end of the accounting period, the balance on the bad debts account is transferred to the profit and loss (P & L) account (like all other expense accounts):

DEBIT	P & L account
CREDIT	Bad debts account

Note. If a customer pays a debt *after* the year end which has already been written off, the double entry will be:

DEBIT	Cash
CREDIT	P & L account

If he pays *before* the year end, then the original entries in the nominal and sales ledgers (in (a) and (b)) are simply reversed.

Example: Bad debts written off

7.5   At 1 October 19X5 a business had total outstanding debts of £8,600. During the year to 30 September 19X6:

(a)   credit sales amounted to £44,000;
(b)   payments from various debtors amounted to £49,000;
(c)   two debts, for £180 and £420 were declared bad. These are to be written off.

Task

Prepare the debtors account and the bad debts accounts for the year.

Solution: Bad debts written off

7.6

DEBTORS

Date	Details	£	Date	Details	£
1.10.X5	Balance b/f	8,600		Cash	49,000
	Sales for the year	44,000	30.9.X6	Bad debts	180
			30.9.X6	Bad debts	420
			30.9.X6	Balance c/d	3,000
		52,600			52,600
	Balance b/d	3,000			

BAD DEBTS

Date	Details	£	Date	Details	£
30.9.X6	Debtors	180	30.9.X6	P & L a/c: bad debts	600
30.9.X6	Debtors	420		written off	
		600			600

7.7 A write off of any bad debt will need the *authorisation* of a senior official in the organisation.

7.8 In the sales ledger, personal accounts of the customers whose debts are bad will be taken off the ledger. The business should then take steps to make sure that it does not sell goods to those customers again.

Provision for doubtful debts: ledger accounting entries

7.9 A provision for doubtful debts is rather different from a bad debt written off. A business might know from past experience that, say, 2% of debtors' balances are unlikely to be collected. It would then be considered prudent to make a *general provision* of 2% of total debtor balances. It may be that no particular customers are regarded as suspect and so it is not possible to write off any individual customer balances as bad debts. The procedure is then to leave the total debtors balances completely untouched, but to open up a provision account by the following entries:

DEBIT Doubtful debts account (expense: P & L account)
CREDIT Provision for doubtful debts

When preparing a balance sheet, the credit balance on the provision account is *deducted* from the total debit balances in the debtors ledger.

7.10 In *subsequent years*, adjustments may be needed to the amount of the provision. The procedure to be followed then is as follows.

Step 1 Calculate the new provision required.

Step 2 Compare it with the existing balance on the provision account (ie the balance b/f from the previous accounting period).

Step 3 Calculate the increase or decrease required.

(a) If a *higher provision* is required now:

DEBIT P & L account
CREDIT Provision for doubtful debts

with the amount of the increase.

(b) If a *lower provision* is needed now than before:

DEBIT Provision for doubtful debts
CREDIT P & L account

with the amount of the decrease.

Example: Provision for doubtful debts

7.11 Alex Gullible has total debtors' balances outstanding at 31 December 19X2 of £28,000. He believes that about 1% of these balances will not be collected and wishes to make an appropriate provision. Before now, he has not made any provision for doubtful debts at all.

On 31 December 19X3 his debtors' balances amount to £40,000. His experience during the year has convinced him that a provision of 5% should be made.

What accounting entries should Alex make on 31 December 19X2 and 31 December 19X3, and what figures for debtors will appear in his balance sheets as at those dates?

Solution: Provision for doubtful debts

7.12   *At 31 December 19X2*

Provision required   = 1% × £28,000 = £280

Alex will make the following entries.

DEBIT	P & L account (doubtful debts)	£280	
CREDIT	Provision for doubtful debts		£280

In the balance sheet debtors will appear as follows under current assets.

	£
Sales ledger balances	28,000
Less provision for doubtful debts	280
	27,720

At 31 December 19X3

Following the procedure described above, Alex will calculate as follows.

	£
Provision required now (5% × £40,000)	2,000
Existing provision	(280)
∴ Additional provision required	1,720

DEBIT	P & L account (doubtful debts)	£1,720	
CREDIT	Provision for doubtful debts		£1,720

Note. The two P&L accounts for bad debt expense and for doubtful debts are often combined.

The provision account will by now appear as follows.

PROVISION FOR DOUBTFUL DEBTS

Date	Details	£	Date	Details	£
19X2			19X2		
31 Dec	Balance c/d	280	31 Dec	P & L account	280
19X3			19X3		
31 Dec	Balance c/d	2,000	1 Jan	Balance b/d	280
			31 Dec	P & L account	1,720
		2,000			2,000
			19X4		
			1 Jan	Balance b/d	2,000

For the balance sheet, debtors will be valued as follows.

	£
Sales ledger balances	40,000
Less provision for doubtful debts	2,000
	38,000

7.13   In practice, it is unnecessary to show the total debtors balances and the provision as separate items in the balance sheet. A balance sheet would normally show only the net figure (£27,720 in 19X2; £38,000 in 19X3).

Bad debts and VAT

7.14   A business can claim relief from value added tax (VAT) on bad debts which are at least six months old (from the time of supply) and which have been written off in the accounts of the business.

7.15   VAT bad debt relief is claimed by deducting the value of VAT on bad debts from the value of output tax (ie VAT on sales) due on the VAT return submitted to HM Customs & Excise for the VAT period in which the relief becomes available.

8 FROM LEDGERS TO FINANCIAL STATEMENTS: AN OVERVIEW

8.1 Ultimately the balance sheet and trading, profit and loss accounts are a summary of the balances on the ledger accounts at any time. It might be useful to recap how a simple business transaction gets to the financial statements.

8.2 In an earlier example, a business received an invoice for £1,800 from an advertising agency, PDQ Media on 28 January 19X6.

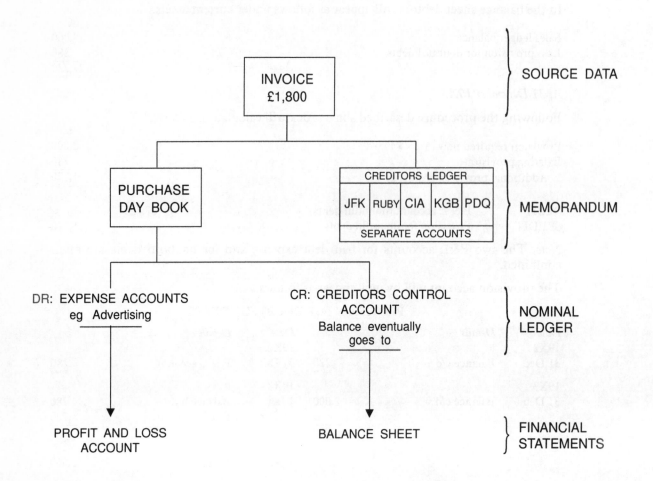

8.3 Let us look again at the ledger account for *advertising expenditure*.

ADVERTISING EXPENSES

Date 19X6	Narrative	Folio	£	Date 19X6	Narrative	Folio	£
3.1	JFK Agency	PL48	2,500	13.1	Refund from JFK	PR271	125
12.1	Ruby, Oswald	PL274	1,500				
21.1	CIA Agency	PL399	1,750				
23.1	KGB Advertising	PL420	1,000				
28.1	PDQ Media	PL732	1,800	31.1	Carried down		8,425
			8,550				8,550
1.2	Brought down		8,425				

8.4 The amount of £8,425 would appear in the profit and loss account for January 19X6. It may be the case that we wish to start a completely *new* accounting period, say for February 19X6. Then we would start up a new ledger account to total our expenses for February 19X6. This is because the profit and loss account is a record of transactions *over a period of time*.

8.5 The balance sheet, on the other hand, describes a *state of affairs at a particular time*. If the invoice remains unpaid at the end of the accounting period, the amount owed will be included within the balance on the creditors control account in the balance sheet. On the other hand, if it is paid by the end of the period, the cash paid will instead be reflected in the balance sheet (because the amount of cash held will be reduced). We do not 'set' balance sheet accounts at zero at the beginning of a new accounting period, as we still own assets and still owe liabilities.

8.6 The nature of entries on each side of the balance sheet and profit and loss account can be summarised as below.

BALANCE SHEET		PROFIT AND LOSS ACCOUNT	
Debit	*Credit*	*Debit*	*Credit*
£	£	£	£
Assets			Income
(What we own)			(What we've earned)
	Liabilities	Expenses	
	(What we owe)	(What we've spent)	

9 FROM LEDGERS TO FINANCIAL STATEMENTS: THE MECHANICS

9.1 It is unlikely that a Central Assessment task will require the preparation of final accounts from the ledgers. However, this technique completes your understanding of double entry, begun at Foundation level. It is reintroduced and revised in depth in Chapter 7, because it is a very important technique when tackling incomplete records, manufacturing accounts or club accounts, all of which are potentially assessable. You will need to prepare final accounts, usually from a set of balances, and to use ledger accounts as workings. You may wish to refer back to this chapter when you reach Chapter 7.

Key points in this chapter

- Source data about a transaction is often captured in a *book of prime entry*, such as a sales day book, a purchases day book or the journal, although there are other books of prime entry too. It is possible that the payroll system could be a book of prime entry.

- Data from the book of prime entry is transferred in total, at the end of each period, to the *nominal ledger* (or *general ledger*).

- The nominal ledger works on the *double entry system*. This means that every business transaction has two aspects, recorded as a debit and a credit.

  o *Debit balances* constitute assets (eg if the business owns a property, or cash, or someone - a debtor - owes money to the business), and expenses (eg for electricity).

  o *Credit balances* are liabilities (eg if the business owes money to someone) and revenue (eg from selling goods).

- For example, if you sell something for £100 in cash the entries are:

  o DEBIT   Cash (ie asset) £100
  o CREDIT   Sales (ie income) £100

- To give another example, if you receive a bill for £100 electricity, the entries are:

  o DEBIT   Electricity expenses £100
  o CREDIT   Electricity company creditor (liability account) £100

- Accounts for revenue and expenses belong to the *profit and loss account*.

- Asset and liability accounts belong to the *balance sheet*.

- Some debts may need to be written off as *bad debts* because there is no real prospect of them being paid. Alternatively or additionally, a *provision for doubtful debts* may be created. Rather than affecting individual customer balances, a provision for doubtful debts recognises the fact that ordinarily a certain proportion of all debts are unlikely to be collected. It is therefore prudent to make such a general 'provision' when calculating the overall profit or loss of the business.

- At suitable intervals, the entries in ledger accounts are totalled and a *balance* is struck. Balances are usually collected in a *trial balance* which is then used as a basis for preparing a profit and loss account and a balance sheet. This technique is dealt with in Chapter 7.

For practice on the points covered in this chapter you should now attempt the Practice Exercises in Session 1 of the Financial Accounting Workbook

2 Classification of assets and fundamental accounting concepts

---

This chapter covers the following topics.

1   Introduction

2   Ways of classifying assets

3   Assets and expenses

4   What are fundamental accounting concepts?

5   The prudence concept

6   The going concern concept

7   The accruals concept or matching concept

8   The consistency concept

9   The materiality concept

10 Historical cost accounting

---

1   INTRODUCTION

1.1   We looked at assets in our examination of the balance sheet in the previous chapter. We know that assets are recorded as debit balances, and they are what a business actually possesses. However, there are a variety of different types of asset. Knowing about these is a requirement for Unit 4: *Recording capital transactions*. It is also relevant to Unit 5: *Preparing financial accounts*.

1.2   Here we discuss briefly the different types of asset that might be encountered in the balance sheet of a business.

2   WAYS OF CLASSIFYING ASSETS

2.1   As an exercise, you might note down all the different kinds of asset that a business might possess. Go back to the previous chapter if you like for some ideas.

Whatever you write down, you can probably find a number of ways of classifying assets. Here are some examples.

Lifetime of an asset

2.2   Assets have varying *estimated useful lives*.

2.3   A building, for example, which a business owns and which it intends to occupy for an indefinite period, is evidently an asset with a long life. You would therefore expect to see that asset represented for many years in the balance sheet of the business. The value given to that asset will change, owing to *depreciation* (discussed in your Unit 4 studies) and *revaluation*, but the asset will be there for a long time.

2.4   An item of plant and machinery will probably have a shorter life in the business, say about four or five years, before it wears out or becomes out of date and must be replaced.

2.5   Some assets have much shorter lives. For example, a company manufacturing goods might keep a small amount of finished goods stocks in its warehouse for a few days before delivery. These are assets. If a snapshot balance sheet were taken of the business, then assets would appear as a debit balance in the balance sheet.

2.6   The lifetime of an asset can affect its *value*. An item of stock, as described in Paragraph 2.5 above, which was still in the warehouse 20 years after it had been made might not be worth anything, except scrap value (unless of course it had become an antique, or a collector's item!). After all, if it cost £100 to make that item of stock, you could hardly show it in the balance sheet at £100 if it could only be sold for £10.

Fixed assets and current assets

2.7   A balance sheet is normally produced every year, and assets are classified by time.

(a)   A *fixed asset* is for continuing use within the business (eg an item of machinery, which makes the products which the business sells). It will have been purchased with this long-term use in mind.

(b)   A *current asset* only has a short lifetime. It is not for continuing use within the business. A debtor should pay within a short period. An item of stock is made to be sold fairly soon.

2.8   As a general rule, the value of an asset ought to *decline with time*. Machinery wears out. A car, for example, loses value with time. The main exception to this rule is freehold property.

Tangible or intangible assets

2.9   When you wrote down a list of assets, you might have only noted down objects that you could touch, see, inspect and manipulate, like cars, machines, buildings, or even stock. These are *tangible* assets.

2.10 Some assets are *intangible*. This means they are not physical, and cannot be touched. Can you think of any intangible assets? Some examples are given below.

2.11 A *patent* is an exclusive right to a design of something. Suppose that you invented some wonderful drug, and you had spent a lot of money in researching and developing it. You would feel that someone who came and copied your invention, selling imitations at a cheaper price, was stealing your invention from you, and making use of your efforts and labour without paying you for it. A patent allows you, for a limited period of time, to protect your investment by stopping other people from copying your invention.

       Patents have only a *limited life* which varies in length between countries.

2.12 *Goodwill* is a very difficult area of accounting, which we will not go into in any detail at this level. Suffice it to say that the concept of goodwill arises out of the idea of a business's reputation.

       For example, assume that Albert Herring runs a fish and chip shop which is popular and has a good reputation. One day, Rick Salmon sets up a competing fish and chip shop next door. Mr Salmon's chip shop is identical in every respect. It is the same size as Albert Herring's, serves fish which are just as fresh, and in fact is identical in every way, down to the crust on the tomato ketchup bottles.

       Yet Albert Herring still receives far more customers, when there is no obvious reason why they should prefer his fish and chips to Rick Salmon's. This is because he has been around for a while, and has a good reputation. If Rick Salmon purchased Albert's shop, but still used Albert's name, Albert's former shop would still attract custom because of its name. The business is worth more (in terms of potential future profits) because of its reputation than it would be if the business's assets were sold individually.

       You might be interested to know that, in the case of limited companies, goodwill such as that which Albert has built up is not recorded in the accounts of Albert's company. On the other hand, if Rick Salmon bought Albert's business, then this extra value would be included in the accounts because it had to be *paid for* and a monetary value can now be put on to it.

2.13 Other intangible assets include copyright, trade marks, even 'brands' (eg Mars bars) in some instances.

Liquidity of assets

2.14 Another way of classifying assets is the degree to which they are, or are intended to be, turned into cash.

       (a) *Fixed assets*, as we have seen, are intended for continuing use within the business and not for re-sale. Only when a business goes bankrupt or is otherwise wound up, does the possible sale value of fixed assets really matter. Even in this case, it might be hard to sell fixed assets, as the market in partly worn out specialist equipment may be limited.

       (b) An item of *finished goods stock* (eg for a motor manufacturer, a newly manufactured car), is not intended to be kept in the business for its continuing use. Ultimately, it is to be sold for cash, or in a credit sale.

       (c) A *debtor* is also an asset (remember, it is a debit and goes to the balance sheet). From the point of view of the business, a debtor is more liquid than an item of stock, simply because it is a financial obligation on someone to pay rather than a physical thing which someone might buy.

(d) A *prepayment* is a payment you have made in advance for something. You are owed the goods or services supplied, and so this is another kind of asset.

(e) *Cash* is the most liquid asset as it can be used for any purpose. In other words, you can use cash to pay the business's electricity bill, pay for raw materials and so on. You cannot, on the other hand, use an item of stock (eg a portion of a manufactured car) to pay the electricity bill. (Barter, which is the exchange of goods for other goods rather than goods for cash, is sometimes practised, but is not the norm.)

2.15 The above can be summarised as follows.

(a) *Fixed assets* are generally illiquid, as it is not intended that they should be sold.

(b) *Current assets* are generally expected to be cash, or realised as cash at some stage.

(i) *Stock* is the least liquid current asset. It might take time to sell an item of stock. There is thus uncertainty that it can be converted into cash quickly.

(ii) A *debt* is a financial obligation. For example, someone has bought something and the debt is the agreed price. A bad debt is a debt which will not be paid. Even so, you can still sue to collect a bad debt, whereas you cannot force someone to buy an item of stock.

(iii) *Cash* is the most liquid asset of all.

3 ASSETS AND EXPENSES

3.1 Both assets and expenses are represented by debit balances, although assets appear in the balance sheet and expenses in the profit and loss account.

3.2 It is possible to confuse assets and expenses, and there are good reasons for avoiding this confusion. After all, suppose that an expense of £100 is incorrectly posted to the balance sheet (ie as an asset).

(a) The profits of the business are £100 more than they would otherwise have been, as expenses have been reduced by £100.

(b) The assets of the business are increased by £100.

3.3 At the AAT Foundation stage, we learned about the difference between *revenue* and *capital* expenditure. Some questions arise about whether to treat certain items as revenue or capital items.

(a) What about research and development expenditure, ie expenditure on developing new products? Should it be taken to the profit and loss account, or should it be treated as an asset in the balance sheet, until the new products are sold?

(b) If you borrow money to buy an item of machinery, do you treat the interest on that loan as capital expenditure?

(c) How do you account for the wear and tear on a fixed asset such as an item of machinery?

3.4 How do you make up your mind? Partly, the treatment of certain items is already decided for you:

(a) by law;

(b) by accounting standards. These are called Statements of Standard Accounting Practice (SSAPs) and (more recently) Financial Reporting Standards (FRSs).

Legal regulations about accounting are included, in the UK, in the Companies Act. Accounting standards are produced by the Accounting Standards Board, made up of members of professional accounting bodies, users and the government. Accounting standards are discussed in more detail in the next chapter.

3.5 The rest if the time, you must answer questions such as those in Paragraph 3.3. by applying the fundamental accounting concepts. For the rest of this chapter, we are going to deal with some of fundamental accounting concepts which *underpin* the law and the accounting standards, and which are embodied in them.

4 WHAT ARE FUNDAMENTAL ACCOUNTING CONCEPTS?

4.1 Accounting practice has developed gradually over a long period of time. Many of its procedures are operated automatically by accounting personnel and these procedures in common use imply the acceptance of certain concepts. These concepts are not necessarily obvious, nor are they the only possible concepts which could be used to build up an accounting framework, but they are the concepts which our current system has ended up being based upon.

4.2 Let us then look at some of the more important concepts which are taken for granted in preparing accounts. One statement of standard accounting practice (SSAP 2 *Disclosure of accounting policies*) describes *four* of these concepts as *fundamental accounting concepts:* they are going concern, prudence, accruals and consistency. These four are also identified as fundamental by the Companies Act 1985, which adds a fifth to the list (the separate valuation principle). But there is no universally agreed list of fundamental concepts, and others besides these have been described as fundamental.

4.3 Here are some concepts for discussion.

(a) The *entity concept*: a business, for accounting purposes, is a separate entity from its owners or managers

(b) The *money measurement concept*: accounts only deal with items to which a monetary value can be attributed

(c) The *separate valuation principle*: each component part of an asset or liability on the balance sheet must be valued separately

(d) The *prudence concept*

(e) The *going concern concept*

(f) The *accruals or matching concept*

(g) The *consistency concept*

(h) The *materiality concept*

Items (d) to (h) are dealt with in detail below.

5 THE PRUDENCE CONCEPT
Centrally assessed 12/95, 6/97

5.1 This concept states that, where alternative procedures or alternative valuations are possible, the one selected should be the one which gives the *most cautious* presentation of the business's financial position or results. Assume, for example, that you were in business making washing machines. Each machine costs £100 to make, but can be sold for £150. Stocks of finished washing machines would be valued in the balance sheet at £100 each. This is one aspect of the prudence concept: to value the machines at £150 would be to anticipate making a profit before the profit had been *realised* (ie obtained in cash or the promise of cash, see below).

5.2 Another aspect of the prudence concept is that, where a *loss* is foreseen, it should be *anticipated* and taken into account immediately. If a business purchases stock for £1,200 but because of a sudden slump in the market only £900 is likely to be received when the stock is sold, the prudence concept states that the stock should be valued at £900. It is not enough to wait until the stock is sold, and then recognise the £300 loss; the loss should be recognised as soon as it is foreseen.

5.3 A profit can be considered to be a *realised* profit when it is in the form of:

(a) cash; or

(b) another asset which has a reasonably certain cash value. This includes amounts owing from debtors, provided that there is a reasonable certainty that the debtors will eventually pay up what they owe.

5.4 Under the prudence concept, as defined by SSAP 2, *revenue* and *profits* are not anticipated, but are included in the profit and loss account only when realised in the form of cash (or of other assets which are certain to be exchanged for cash in the near future). All known *expenses* and *losses* should be included in the profit and loss account whether the amount of these is known with certainty or a best estimate is used in the light of the information available.

5.5 Some examples might help to explain the application of the prudence concept.

(a) A company begins trading on 1 January 19X5 and sells goods for £100,000 during the year to 31 December. At 31 December there are debts outstanding of £15,000. Of these, the company is now doubtful whether £6,000 will ever be paid.

The company should make a *provision for doubtful debts* of £6,000. Sales for 19X5 will be shown in the profit and loss account at their full value of £100,000, but the provision for doubtful debts would be a charge of £6,000. Because there is some uncertainty that the sales will be realised in the form of cash, the prudence concept dictates that the £6,000 should not be included in the profit for the year.

(b) Samson Feeble trades as a carpenter. He has undertaken to make a range of kitchen furniture for a customer at an agreed price of £1,000. At the end of Samson's accounting year the job is unfinished (being two-thirds complete) and the following information has been assembled.

	£
Costs incurred in making the furniture to date	800
Further estimated costs to completion of the job	400
Total cost	1,200

The incomplete job represents *work in progress* at the end of the year which is an asset, like stock. Its cost to date is £800, but by the time the job is completed Samson will have made a loss of £200.

The full £200 loss should be charged against profits of the current year. The value of work in progress at the year end should be its *net realisable value*, which is lower than its cost. The net realisable value can be calculated in either of two ways.

	(i)			*(ii)*
	£			£
Eventual sales value	1,000	Work in progress at cost		800
Less further costs to		Less loss foreseen		200
completion in order to make				
the sale	400			
Net realisable value	600			600

5.6 It is generally agreed that sales revenue should only be 'realised' and so 'recognised' in the trading, profit and loss account when:

(a) the sale transaction is for a *specific quantity* of goods at a known price, so that the sales value of the transaction is known for certain;

(b) the sale transaction has been *completed*, or else it is certain that it will be completed (eg in the case of long-term construction work under contract, when the job is well under way but not yet finished by the end of an accounting period);

(c) the *critical event* in the sale transaction has occurred. The critical event is the event after which either:

(i) it becomes virtually certain that cash will eventually be received from the customer; or

      (ii)   cash is actually received.

5.7   Usually, revenue is 'recognised' either:

    (a)   when a *cash sale* is made; or

    (b)   when the customer *promises to pay* on or before a specified future date, and the debt is legally enforceable.

    The prudence concept is applied here in the sense that revenue should not be anticipated, and should not be included in the trading, profit and loss account before it is reasonably certain that it will arise.

Example: The prudence concept

5.8   Given that prudence is the main consideration, discuss under what circumstances, if any, revenue might be recognised at the following stages of a sale.

    (a)   Goods have been acquired by the business which it confidently expects to resell very quickly.

    (b)   A customer places a firm order for goods.

    (c)   Goods are delivered to the customer.

    (d)   The customer is invoiced for goods.

    (e)   The customer pays for the goods.

    (f)   The customer's cheque in payment for the goods has been cleared by the bank.

Solution: The prudence concept

5.9   (a)   A sale must never be recognised before the goods have even been ordered. There is no certainty about the value of the sale, nor when it will take place, even if it is virtually certain that goods will be sold.

    (b)   A sale should not be recognised when the customer places an order. Even though the order will be for a specific quantity of goods at a specific price, it is not yet certain that the sale transaction will go through. The customer may cancel the order, or the supplier might be unable to deliver the goods as ordered.

    (c)   A sale will be recognised when delivery of the goods is made only if:

        (i)   the sale is for cash, and so the cash is received at the same time; or

        (ii)   the sale is on credit and the customer accepts delivery (eg by signing a delivery note).

    (d)   The critical event for a credit sale is usually the dispatch of an invoice to the customer. There is then a legally enforceable debt, payable on specified terms, for a completed sale transaction.

    (e)   The critical event for a cash sale is when delivery takes place and when cash is received; both usually take place at the same time.

        It would be excessively 'cautious' to await cash payment for a credit sale transaction before recognising the sale, unless the customer is a high credit risk and there is a serious doubt about his ability or intention to pay.

    (f)   It would also normally be over-cautious to wait for clearance of the customer's cheques before recognising sales revenue. Such a precaution would only be justified in cases where there is a very high risk of the bank refusing to honour the cheque.

5.10   You should note that, following SSAP 2, if the prudence concept and the accruals concept (see below) conflict, the *prudence concept prevails.*

6   THE GOING CONCERN CONCEPT

6.1   The going concern concept implies that the business will continue in operational existence for the foreseeable future, and that there is no intention to put the company into liquidation or to make drastic cutbacks to the scale of operations.

6.2   The main significance of the going concern concept is that the assets of the business should not be valued at their 'break-up' value, which is the amount that they would sell for if they were sold off piecemeal and the business were thus broken up.

6.3   Suppose, for example, that Emma acquires a T-shirt-printing machine at a cost of £60,000. The asset has an estimated life of six years, and it is normal to write off the cost of the asset to the profit and loss account over this time (as we will see in Chapter 4). In this case a depreciation cost of £10,000 per annum will be charged.

6.4   Using the going concern concept, it would be presumed that the business will continue its operations and so the asset will live out its full six years in use. A depreciation charge of £10,000 will be made each year, and the value of the asset in the balance sheet will be its cost less the accumulated amount of depreciation charged to date. After one year, the net book value of the asset would therefore be £(60,000 − 10,000) = £50,000, after two years it would be £40,000, after three years £30,000 etc, until it has been written down to a value of 0 after 6 years.

6.5   Now suppose that this asset has no other operational use outside the business, and in a forced sale it would only sell for scrap. After one year of operation, its scrap value might be, say, £8,000. What would the net book value be after one year?

6.6   The net book value of the asset, applying the going concern concept, would be £50,000 after one year, but its immediate sell-off value only £8,000. It might be argued that the asset is over-valued at £50,000 and that it should be written down to its break-up value (ie in the balance sheet it should be shown at £8,000 and the balance of its cost should be treated as an expense). However, provided that the going concern concept is valid, so that the asset will continue to be used and will not be sold, it is appropriate accounting practice to value the asset at its net book value.

7   THE ACCRUALS CONCEPT OR MATCHING CONCEPT
Centrally assessed 6/95, 12/95, 12/96

7.1   The accruals or 'matching' concept states that, in computing profit, revenue earned must be *matched* against the expenditure incurred in earning it. This can be best illustrated by an example.

Example: Accruals basis

7.2   Brenda has a business importing and selling model Corgi dogs. In May 19X9, she makes the following purchases and sales.

Purchases

Invoice date	Number	Invoiced cost £	Invoice paid
7.5.X9	20	100	1.6.X9

Sales

Invoice date	Number	Invoice value £	Invoice paid
8.5.X9	4	40	1.6.X9
12.5.X9	6	60	1.6.X9
23.5.X9	10	100	1.7.X9

What is Brenda's profit and loss account for May?

Solution : Accruals basis

		£
7.3	*Cash basis*	
	Sales	-
	Purchases	-
	Profit/loss	-
	Accruals basis	
	Sales (£40 + £60 + £100)	200
	Purchases	100
	Profit	100

7.4 If, furthermore, Brenda had only sold eighteen Corgis, it would have been incorrect to charge her profit and loss account with the cost of twenty Corgis, as she still has two Corgis in stock. If she intends to sell them in June she is likely to make a profit on the sale. Therefore, only the purchase cost of eighteen Corgis (£90) should be matched with her sales revenue, leaving her with a profit of £90.

Her balance sheet would therefore look like this.

	£
Assets	
Stock (at cost, ie 2 × £5)	10
Debtors (18 × £10)	180
	190
Liabilities	
Creditors	100
	90
Proprietor's capital (profit for the period)	90

7.5 Obviously, the accruals basis gives a truer picture than the cash basis. Brenda has no cash to show for her efforts until June but her customers are legally bound to pay her and she is legally bound to pay for her purchases.

Her balance sheet as at 31 May 19X9 would therefore show her assets and liabilities as follows.

	£
Assets: Debtors (£40 + £60 + £100)	200
Liabilities: Creditors	100
Net assets	100
Proprietor's capital	100

7.6 If, however Brenda had decided to give up selling Corgis, then the going concern concept (see Section 6 above) would no longer apply and the value of the two Corgis in the balance sheet would be a 'break-up' valuation rather than cost, ie the amount that would be obtained by selling the stock following break-up or liquidation of the business. Similarly, if the two unsold Corgis were now unlikely to be sold at more than their cost of £5 each (say, because of damage or a fall in demand) then they should be recorded on the balance sheet at their *net realisable value* (ie the likely eventual sales price less any expenses incurred to make them saleable, eg paint) rather than cost. This shows the application of the prudence concept.

7.7 In this example, the concepts of going concern and matching are linked. Because the business is assumed to be a going concern it is possible to carry forward the cost of the unsold Corgis as a charge against profits of the next period.

The accruals concept defined

7.8 Under the 'accruals' or 'matching' concept, as defined by SSAP 2 (and given legal recognition by the Companies Act), revenues and costs are *accrued* (that is, recognised as they are earned or incurred, not as money is received or paid), matched with one another if they are related to each other, and dealt with in the profit and loss account of the period to which they relate. This means that revenue and profits dealt with in the profit and loss account of the period are *matched* with associated costs and expenses by including the costs incurred in earning them in the same accounting period. Businesses must take credit for sales and purchases when made, rather than when paid for, and they must also carry unsold stock forward in the balance sheet rather than deduct its cost from profit for the period.

8 THE CONSISTENCY CONCEPT
Centrally assessed 12/95

8.1 Accounting is not an exact science. There are many areas in which judgement must be used to calculate or estimate the money values of items appearing in accounts. Over the years certain procedures and principles have come to be recognised as good accounting practice, but within these limits there are often various acceptable methods of accounting for similar items.

8.2 The *consistency concept* states that in preparing accounts consistency should be observed in two respects.

(a) *Similar items* within a single set of accounts should be given similar accounting treatment.

(b) The same treatment should be applied *from one period to another* in accounting for similar items. This allows valid comparisons to be made from one period to the next.

8.3 To understand the importance of the consistency concept, consider how meaningless asset values would be to a reader of a set of accounts if the basis on which they were decided changed completely from one year to the next - one year purchased cost, the next replacement cost (the cost of buying a new one), the next market value (sales value).

9 THE MATERIALITY CONCEPT
Centrally assessed 12/94, 6/95, 12/96

9.1 An error which is too trivial to affect anyone's understanding of accounting reports is referred to as *immaterial*. In preparing accounts it is important to ask the following questions.

(a) Do materiality considerations apply? (You will pay the *exact* amount of a purchase invoice, for example, no matter how large it is. You would not *round* up or down, or approximate.)

(b) If they do, what is material and what is not? Time and money should not be wasted in the pursuit of *excessive detail*.

9.2 Determining whether or not an item is material is a very *subjective* exercise. There is no absolute measure of materiality. It is common to apply a convenient rule of thumb (for example to define material items as those with a value greater than 5% of the net profit disclosed by the accounts). But some items disclosed in accounts are regarded as particularly sensitive and even a very small misstatement of such an item would be regarded as a material error. An example in the accounts of a limited company might be the amounts paid to directors of the company.

9.3 Whether an item is judged as material or immaterial may affect its treatment in the accounts. For example, the profit and loss account of a business will show the expenses incurred by the business grouped under suitable headings (heating and lighting expenses, rent and rates expenses etc); but in the case of very small expenses it may be appropriate to lump them together under a heading such as 'sundry expenses', because a more detailed breakdown would be unhelpful for such immaterial amounts.

9.4   In assessing whether or not an item is material, it is not only the amount of the item which needs to be considered. The *context* is also important.

   (a) If a balance sheet shows fixed assets of £2 million and stocks of £30,000, an error of £20,000 in the depreciation calculations might not be regarded as material, whereas an error of £20,000 in the stock valuation probably would be. In other words, the total of which the erroneous item forms part must be considered.

   (b) If a business has a bank loan of £50,000 and a £55,000 balance on bank deposit account, it might well be regarded as a material misstatement if these two amounts were displayed on the balance sheet netted off as 'cash at bank £5,000'. In other words, incorrect presentation may amount to material misstatement even if there is no monetary error.

10   HISTORICAL COST ACCOUNTING

10.1   Accounting concepts are part of the theoretical framework on which accounting practice is based. It is worth looking at one further general point: the problem of attributing monetary values to the items which appear in accounts.

10.2   A basic principle of accounting (some writers include it in the list of fundamental accounting concepts) is that transactions are normally stated in accounts at their historical amount.

10.3   The *historical cost convention*, as it is called, has a number of implications.

   (a) Transactions are stated at their *value when they occurred*. This means, for example, that the cost of goods sold is not suddenly increased at the end of the year.

   (b) Assets are stated at their *historical cost*. In other words, the value of an asset in a balance sheet is based on the price that was paid for it.

10.4   An important advantage of this convention is that there is usually *objective*, documentary evidence to prove the purchase price of an asset, or amounts paid as expenses.

10.5   In general, accountants prefer to deal with objective costs, rather than with estimated values. This is because valuations tend to be subjective and to vary according to what the valuation is for. There are some problems with the principle of historical cost.

   (a) The wearing out of assets over time
   (b) The increase in market value of property
   (c) Inflation

There may be other problems you can think of.

10.6   For example, suppose that a company acquires a machine to manufacture its products. The machine has an expected useful life of four years. At the end of two years the company is preparing a balance sheet and has to decide what monetary amount to attribute to the asset. Numerous possibilities might be considered.

   (a) The original cost (historical cost) of the machine

   (b) Half of the historical cost, on the ground that half of its useful life has expired

   (c) The amount the machine might fetch on the secondhand market

   (d) The amount it would cost to replace the machine with an identical machine

   (e) The amount it would cost to replace the machine with a more modern machine incorporating the technological advances of the previous two years

   (f) The machine's economic value, ie the amount of the profits it is expected to generate for the company during its remaining life

10.7 All of these valuations have something to recommend them, but the great advantage of the first two, (a) and (b), is that they are based on a figure (the machine's historical cost) which is objectively verifiable.

Key points in this chapter

- There are many different kinds of assets.

  o *Fixed* and *current* assets
  o *Tangible* and *intangible* assets

- Whether a debit balance represents an *asset* or *expense* is not always immediately apparent.

- In preparing financial statements, certain *fundamental concepts* are adopted as a framework. From the many concepts which might be identified, we have examined some of particular importance.

  o *Prudence*: a cautious approach is advised
  o *Going concern*: the business is expected to stay 'in business'
  o *Accruals*: revenues and costs should be matched in the same time period
  o *Consistency*: like items should be treated in a like way
  o *Materiality*: in some cases, attention to detail can obscure the 'big picture'

For practice on the points covered in this chapter you should now attempt the Practice Exercises in Session 2 of the Financial Accounting Workbook

3 The general function and status of SSAPs and FRSs

This chapter covers the following topics.

1 **The development of accounting standards**

2 **UK accounting standards**

3 **International accounting standards**

---

1   THE DEVELOPMENT OF ACCOUNTING STANDARDS

1.1   Up until 1970, the basic conventions used in preparing financial reports had evolved over many years of this century. They were essentially the product of the 'collective experience' of practising accountants and were not founded upon a single, comprehensive theory of accounting. Conformity in reporting methods was not seriously encouraged until *accounting standards* were first introduced in the 1970s.

1.2   An *accounting standard* is a rule or set of rules which prescribes the method (or methods) by which accounts should be prepared and presented. These 'working regulations' are issued by a national or international body of the accountancy profession.

1.3   From 1970 until July 1990 accounting standards were formulated and issued by the *Accounting Standards Committee* (ASC). The standards were called Statements of Standard Accounting Practice (SSAPs). The ASC was set up in 1970 as a joint committee of members of the six major accountancy bodies in Britain, the constituent members of the Consultative Committee of Accountancy Bodies (CCAB).

1.4   In 1987 the CCAB established a review committee under the chairmanship of Sir Ron Dearing and its report *The Making of Accounting Standards* was published in September 1988. Its conclusions were that the arrangements then in operation, where 21 unpaid ASC members met for one half-day once a month to discuss new standards, were no longer adequate to produce timely and authoritative pronouncements.

1.5   The Dearing Committee proposed the following arrangements which were put into effect on 1 August 1990, at which time the ASC was disbanded.

(a)   The *Financial Reporting Council (FRC)* was created to cover a wide constituency of interests at a high level. It guides the standard-setting body (see (b) below) on policy and it ensures that the standard-setting body is properly financed. The FRC also funds and oversees the Review Panel (see (d) below). It has about 25 members drawn from users, preparers and auditors of accounts.

(b)   The task of devising standards is now carried out by the *Accounting Standards Board (ASB)*. The ASB can issue standards on its own behalf (with a two-thirds majority), rather than requiring the approval of all the CCAB bodies as had been the case with new SSAPs. The standards produced by the ASB are called Financial Reporting Standards (FRSs) and these will be discussed later. The ASB adopted all the SSAPs in force as at 1 August 1990, but these are gradually being replaced by FRSs over time.

(c)   The *Urgent Issues Task Force (UITF)* is an offshoot of the ASB whose function it is to tackle urgent matters not covered by existing standards, and for which, given the urgency, the normal standard setting process would not be practicable.

(d)   The *Financial Reporting Review Panel* is concerned with the examination and questioning of departures from accounting standards by large companies. It can take companies to court to force them to revise their accounts.

1.6   The structure of the standard-setting framework can be seen in the following diagram.

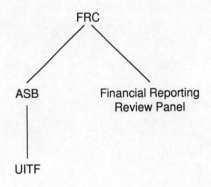

2   UK ACCOUNTING STANDARDS

Legal status

2.1   The Companies Act 1985 requires companies to include a note to the accounts stating that the accounts have been prepared in accordance with applicable accounting standards or, alternatively, giving details of material departures from those standards, with reasons. The Review Panel and the Secretary of State for Trade and Industry have the power to apply to the court for revision of the accounts where non-compliance is not justified. These provisions mean that accounting standards have the force of law, even though accounting standards are not *required* by law.

Statements of Standard Accounting Practice (SSAPs)

2.2   Below is a list of the UK SSAPs in force at the time of writing (August 1997). You do not need to learn this list; it is provided to give you an indication of the aspects of financial reporting to which SSAPs apply. The gaps in the list represent standards which were either withdrawn because of acute unpopularity or replaced by new standards (particularly FRSs, see below).

Number	*Title*
SSAP 1	Accounting for associated companies
SSAP 2	Disclosure of accounting policies
SSAP 3	Earnings per share
SSAP 4	Accounting for government grants
SSAP 5	Accounting for value added tax
SSAP 8	The treatment of taxation under the imputation system in the accounts of companies
SSAP 9	Stocks and long-term contracts
SSAP 12	Accounting for depreciation
SSAP 13	Accounting for research and development
SSAP 15	Accounting for deferred tax
SSAP 17	Accounting for post balance sheet events
SSAP 18	Accounting for contingencies
SSAP 19	Accounting for investment properties
SSAP 20	Foreign currency translation
SSAP 21	Accounting for leases and hire purchase contracts
SSAP 22	Accounting for goodwill
SSAP 24	Accounting for pension costs
SSAP 25	Segmental reporting

2.3   You will only be concerned with a few of these standards in this text, namely 2, 5, 9, 12, 13 and 21.

Financial Reporting Standards (FRSs)

2.4   The ASB's consultative process leads to the setting of Financial Reporting Standards. To produce an FRS, first a working Discussion Draft (DD) is published to stimulate debate and feedback from interested people. The DD, as a result of this process, is converted into a Financial Reporting Exposure Draft (FRED). When final comments on the FRED have been received, then the FRS is produced. This process is demonstrated by the following diagram.

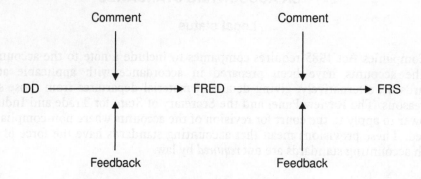

2.5   The following FRSs have been published by the ASB.

Number	Title
FRS 1	Cash flow statements
FRS 2	Accounting for subsidiary undertakings
FRS 3	Reporting financial performance
FRS 4	Capital instruments
FRS 5	Reporting the substance of transactions
FRS 6	Acquisitions and mergers
FRS 7	Fair values in acquisition accounting
FRS 8	Related party disclosures

2.6   These FRSs will not concern you in your studies for Units 4 and 5.

Statement of Aims

2.7   The ASB's draft *Statement of Aims* is a very brief document which lays out the philosophy behind the standard setting process envisaged by the ASB. It is reproduced in full here as it is an important document.

'Aims

The aims of the Accounting Standards Board (the Board) are to establish and improve standards of financial accounting and reporting, for the benefit of users, preparers and auditors of financial information.

Achieving the aims

The Board intends to achieve its aims by:

(a)   Developing principles to guide it in establishing standards and to provide a framework within which others can exercise judgement in resolving accounting issues.

(b)   Issuing new accounting standards, or amending existing ones, in response to evolving business practices, new economic developments and deficiencies being identified in current practice.

(c)   Addressing urgent issues promptly.

Fundamental guidelines

(a)   To be objective and to ensure that the information resulting from the application of accounting standards faithfully represents the underlying commercial activity. Such information should be neutral in the sense that it is free from any form of bias intended to influence users in a particular direction and should not be designed to favour any group of users or preparers.

(b)   To ensure that accounting standards are clearly expressed and supported by a reasoned analysis of the issues.

(c)   To determine what should be incorporated in accounting standards based on research, public consultation and careful deliberation about the usefulness of the resulting information.

(d)   To ensure that through a process of regular communication, accounting standards are produced with due regard to international developments.

(e) To ensure that there is consistency both from one accounting standard to another and between accounting standards and company law.

(f) To issue accounting standards only when the expected benefits exceed the perceived costs. The Board recognises that reliable cost/benefit calculations are seldom possible. However, it will always assess the need for standards in terms of the significance and extent of the problem being addressed and will choose the standard which appears to be most effective in cost/benefit terms.

(g) To take account of the desire of the financial community for evolutionary rather than revolutionary change in the reporting process where this is consistent with the objectives outlined above.'

2.8 SSAPs and FRSs apply to all financial accounts which are 'intended to give a true and fair view of the financial position and profit and loss'. A standard may, however, apply only to certain companies, eg companies 'listed' on a Stock Exchange.

2.9 Although there are some areas where the contents of SSAPs and FRSs overlap with company law, standards are detailed working regulations within the framework of government legislation, and they cover areas in which the law is silent. The accountancy profession prefers to make its own rules for self-regulation, rather than to have rules imposed by law.

2.10 The Companies Act 1985 states that a departure from any of its provisions is permissible if a provision is inconsistent with the 'true and fair view' (a term not properly defined in law, so use your common sense). Some accounting standards recommend departure from legal rules on the basis of 'true and fair', but legal opinion feels that, in any case, following accounting standards will also tend to make accounts 'true and fair'.

2.11 To enforce SSAPs and FRSs, the CCAB bodies require their members:

(a) to disclose and explain in the accounts any significant departure from the provisions of UK standards; and

(b) to disclose in the accounts the financial effect of any such departures.

Standards apply mainly to private sector bodies, but they are also used in the public sector, where applicable.

2.12 A standard will choose one possible treatment (or perhaps two) from many which are available as the best practice to be followed. SSAPs were working regulations for practical application and they were perhaps been developed rather haphazardly without a clear, underlying rationale and *conceptual framework* (see below).

The advantages and disadvantages of accounting standards

2.13 SSAPs and FRSs have the following *advantages*.

(a) They reduce or eliminate confusing variations in the methods used to prepare accounts.

(b) They provide a focal point for debate and discussions about accounting practice.

(c) They oblige companies to disclose the accounting policies used in the preparation of accounts.

(d) They are a less rigid alternative to enforcing conformity by means of legislation.

(e) They have obliged companies to disclose more accounting information than they would otherwise have done if standards did not exist.

2.14 The *disadvantages* of accounting standards are as follows.

(a) A set of rules which give backing to one method of preparing accounts might be inappropriate in some circumstances. For example SSAP 12 on depreciation was inappropriate for investment properties (in this case, pressure from the property industry secured an exemption from SSAP 12, and SSAP 19 was later issued to deal with this specific case).

(b)   Standards have in the past been subject to lobbying or government pressure. For example, the first exposure draft on accounting for research and development was revised as a result of pressure from the aerospace and electronics industries.

(c)   SSAPs were not based on a conceptual framework of accounting but the ASB is committed to rectifying this (see below).

(d)   Although the ASC invited comments and discussions, user groups were not directly involved in the creation of SSAPs; there is a fuller consultative process with FRSs and user groups are more directly involved.

(e)   There may be a trend towards rigidity, and away from flexibility in applying the rules. Some commentators feel that professional judgement should be used on technical matters.

Conceptual framework

2.15   A *conceptual framework* is a statement of generally accepted theoretical principles which form the frame of reference for financial reporting. The ASC, when it existed, developed SSAPs in a haphazard manner as working solutions to practical problems with no underlying *conceptual framework*.

2.16   In contrast, the ASB produced an exposure draft of a *Statement of Principles* which when completed will represent the conceptual framework on which all future accounting standards will be based. This includes such matters as how assets and liabilities are defined, when they should be included in the accounts and so on.

3   INTERNATIONAL ACCOUNTING STANDARDS

3.1   The International Accounting Standards Committee (IASC) was set up in June 1973 in an attempt to co-ordinate the development of international accounting standards. It includes representatives from many countries throughout the world, including the USA and the UK.

3.2   International accounting standards are not intended to override local regulations. In the UK, however, the ASB has expressed its support for international accounting standards by incorporating them within the UK standards and seeking comments within the UK on IASC proposals.

Key points in this chapter

- Accounting standards were developed to give *consistency* to financial reporting.

- Most accounting standards are called *SSAPs* (Statements of Standard Accounting Practice), but these are gradually being replaced by *FRSs* (Financial Reporting Standards).

- Accounting standards are *reinforced* by the law, but they are not *required* by it.

For practice on the points covered in this chapter you should now attempt the Practice Exercises in Session 3 of the Financial Accounting Workbook

Part B
Recording capital transactions

4 Unit 4: Recording capital transactions

This chapter covers the following topics.

1 **Fixed assets: the basics**

2 **Depreciation**

3 **Purchase and sale of fixed assets**

4 **The fixed assets register**

5 **Authorisation and control**

---

1 FIXED ASSETS: THE BASICS

1.1 A fixed asset is one which is acquired and retained in the business with a view to earning profits and not merely turning into cash. It is normally used over more than one accounting period. Here are some examples of fixed assets.

 (a) Motor vehicles
 (b) Plant and machinery
 (c) Fixtures and fittings
 (d) Land and buildings

1.2 Fixed assets are to be distinguished from *stocks* which we buy or make in order to sell. Stocks are *current* assets, along with cash and amounts owed to us by debtors.

Capital and revenue expenditure
Centrally assessed 6/94 - 6/97

1.3 *Capital expenditure* is expenditure which results in the acquisition of fixed assets, or an improvement in their earning capacity.

 (a) Capital expenditure is not charged as an expense in the profit and loss account of a business enterprise, although a *depreciation charge* will usually be made to write off the capital expenditure gradually over time (see Section 2 of this chapter). Depreciation charges are expenses in the profit and loss account.

 (b) Capital expenditure on fixed assets results in the appearance of a fixed asset in the *balance sheet* of the business.

 Special methods of accounting for capital expenditure apply in local authorities and in some other public sector organisations. These are not explained further here.

1.4 *Revenue expenditure* is expenditure which is incurred for either of the following reasons.

 (a) For the *purpose of the trade* of the business. This includes expenditure classified as selling and distribution expenses, administration expenses and finance charges.

 (b) To maintain the existing *earning capacity* of fixed assets.

1.5 Revenue expenditure is charged to the *profit and loss account* of a period, provided that it relates to the trading activity and sales of that particular period. For example, if a business buys ten widgets for £200 (£20 each) and sells eight of them during an accounting period, it will have two widgets left in stock at the end of the period. The full £200 is revenue expenditure but only £160 is a cost of goods sold during the period. The remaining £40 (cost of two units) will be included in the balance sheet in the stock of goods held, ie as a current asset valued at £40.

1.6 Suppose that a business purchases a building for £30,000. It then adds an extension to the building at a cost of £10,000. The building needs to have a few broken windows mended, its floors polished and some missing roof tiles replaced. These cleaning and maintenance jobs cost £900.

 In the example, the original purchase (£30,000) and the cost of the extension (£10,000) are capital expenditures, because they are incurred to acquire and then improve a fixed asset. The other costs of £900 are revenue expenditure, because these merely maintain the building and thus the 'earning capacity' of the building.

Capital income and revenue income

1.7 *Capital income* is the proceeds from the sale of non-trading assets (ie proceeds from the sale of fixed assets, including fixed asset investments). The profits (or losses) from the sale of fixed assets are included in the profit and loss account of a business, for the accounting period in which the sale takes place.

1.8 *Revenue income* is derived from the following sources.

    (a) The sale of trading assets

    (b) Interest and dividends received from investments held by the business

Other capital transactions

1.9 The categorisation of capital and revenue items given above does not mention raising additional capital from the owner(s) of the business, or raising and repaying loans. These are transactions which either:

    (a) add to the cash assets of the business, thereby creating a corresponding liability (capital or loan); or

    (b) when a loan is repaid, reduce the liabilities (loan) and the assets (cash) of the business.

None of these transactions would be reported through the profit and loss account.

Why is the distinction important?

1.10 Revenue expenditure results from the purchase of goods and services that will either:

    (a) be used fully in the accounting period in which they are purchased, and so be a cost or expense in the trading, profit and loss account; or

    (b) result in a current asset as at the end of the accounting period because the goods or services have not yet been consumed or made use of. The current asset would be shown in the balance sheet and is not yet a cost or expense in the trading, profit and loss account.

1.11 Capital expenditure results in the purchase or improvement of fixed assets, which are assets that will provide benefits to the business in more than one accounting period, and which are not acquired with a view to being resold in the normal course of trade. The cost of purchased fixed assets is not charged in full to the trading, profit and loss account of the period in which the purchase occurs. Instead, the fixed asset is gradually depreciated over a number of accounting periods.

1.12 Since revenue items and capital items are accounted for in different ways, the correct and consistent calculation of profit for any accounting period depends on the correct and consistent classification of items as revenue or capital.

Materiality

1.13 Many small value assets, although purchased for continuing use in the business, will not be recorded as assets but will instead be written off directly as an expense when purchased. An obvious example would be a box of pencils or a set of file dividers. Clearly you would not bother to capitalise such items and then calculate depreciation on them at the year end!

1.14 The decision as to whether such items are 'small enough' to be written off or 'large enough' to be capitalised is generally clear cut. However, what about borderline items, such as a waste paper basket, a set of 'in-trays', or some software for the computer?

1.15 The decision taken has to depend on whether or not the amount is *material*, that is whether it has a significant effect on the financial statements. Something that is material to a small organisation may not be material to a large one.

Self constructed assets

1.16 Where a business builds it own fixed asset (eg a builder might build his own office), then all the costs involved in building the asset should be included in the recorded cost of the fixed asset. These costs will include raw materials, but also labour costs and related overhead costs. This treatment means that assets which are self-constructed are treated in a similar way as purchased fixed assets (where all such costs are included in the purchase price of the asset).

2   DEPRECIATION

Centrally assessed 6/94 - 6/97

Introduction

2.1 Nearly every fixed asset eventually *wears out* over time, the only exception being freehold land. Machines, cars and other vehicles, fixtures and fittings and even buildings do not last forever.

2.2 When a business acquires a fixed asset, it will have some idea about how long its useful life will be, and might decide to do one of two things.

(a) It may keep on using the fixed asset until it becomes completely worn out, useless and worthless.

(b) Alternatively, the business might decide to sell off the fixed asset at the end of its useful life either by selling it as a second-hand item or as scrap.

2.3 Since a fixed asset has a cost, and a limited useful life, and its value eventually declines, it follows that a charge should be made in the trading, profit and loss account to reflect the use that is made of the asset by the business. This charge is called *depreciation*.

2.4 Suppose that a business buys a machine for £40,000. Its expected life is four years, and at the end of that time it is expected to be worthless. Since the fixed asset is used to make profits for four years, it would be reasonable to charge the cost of the asset over those four years (perhaps by charging £10,000 per annum) so that at the end of the four years the total cost of £40,000 would have been charged against profits.

2.5 Indeed, one way of defining depreciation is to describe it as a means of spreading the cost of a fixed asset over its useful life, thereby matching the cost against the full period during which it earns profits for the business.

2.6 A better definition of depreciation is given by SSAP 12 *Accounting for depreciation*.

'Depreciation is the measure of the wearing out, consumption or other reduction in the useful economic life of a fixed asset, whether arising from use, (passage of) time or obsolescence through technological or market changes. Depreciation should be allocated so as to charge a fair proportion of cost or valuation of the asset to each accounting period expected to benefit from its use.'

2.7 This definition makes two important points.

(a) Depreciation is a measure of the *wearing out* of a fixed asset through use, time or obsolescence.

(b) Depreciation charges should be *spread fairly* over a fixed asset's life, and so allocated to the accounting periods which are expected to benefit (ie make profits) from the asset's use.

(*Note*. 'Amortisation' means writing off and is therefore another term which represents depreciation. A wasting asset is a fixed asset which wastes away through use, and the term is applied to mines, which are depleted both physically and in value as their resources are dug out and taken away.)

The total charge for depreciation

2.8 The total amount to be charged over the life of a fixed asset (the depreciable amount) is usually its cost less any expected 'residual' sales value or disposal value at the end of the asset's life.

 (a) A fixed asset costing £20,000 which has an expected life of five years and an expected residual value of nil should be depreciated by £20,000 in total over the five year period.

 (b) A fixed asset costing £20,000 which has an expected life of five years and an expected residual value of £3,000 should be depreciated by £17,000 in total over the five year period.

Depreciation in the accounts of a business

2.9 When a fixed asset is depreciated, two things must be accounted for, one in the profit and loss account and one in the balance sheet.

 (a) The charge for depreciation is a *cost* or *expense* of the accounting period. For the time being, we shall charge depreciation as an expense in the profit and loss account.

 (b) At the same time, the fixed asset is wearing out and diminishing in value, and so the value of the fixed asset in the balance sheet must be reduced by the amount of depreciation charged. The balance sheet value of the fixed asset will be its *net book value* which is the value net of depreciation in the books of account of the business. Note that the 'net book value' is *not* the same as the 'market value' of the asset.

2.10 The amount of depreciation deducted from the cost of a fixed asset to arrive at its net book value will build up (or 'accumulate') over time, as more depreciation is charged in each successive accounting period. This accumulated depreciation is a 'provision' because it provides for the fall in value of the fixed asset. The term 'provision for depreciation' refers to the 'accumulated depreciation' of a fixed asset.

Example: Depreciation

2.11 A fixed asset costing £40,000 has an expected life of four years and an estimated residual value of nil. It might be depreciated by £10,000 per annum.

	Depreciation charge for the year (P & L a/c) (A) £	Accumulated depreciation at end of year (B) £	Cost of the asset (C) £	Net book value at end of year (C–B) £
At beginning of its life	-	-	40,000	40,000
Year 1	10,000	10,000	40,000	30,000
Year 2	10,000	20,000	40,000	20,000
Year 3	10,000	30,000	40,000	10,000
Year 4	10,000	40,000	40,000	0
	40,000			

At the end of year 4, the full £40,000 of depreciation charges have been made in the profit and loss accounts of the four years. The net book value of the fixed asset is now nil. In theory (although perhaps not in practice) the business will no longer use the fixed asset, which would now need replacing.

Methods of depreciation

2.12 There are several different methods of depreciation. Of these, the two most commonly used are:

(a)   the straight line method; and

(b)   the reducing balance method.

The straight line method

2.13   This is the most commonly used method of all. The total depreciable amount is charged in *equal instalments* to each accounting period over the expected useful life of the asset. In this way, the net book value of the fixed asset declines at a steady rate, or in a 'straight line' over time.

2.14   The annual depreciation charge is calculated as:

$$\frac{\text{Cost of asset minus residual value}}{\text{Expected useful life of the asset}}$$

2.15   Examples of straight line depreciation are as follows.

(a)   A fixed asset costing £20,000 with an estimated life of ten years and no residual value would be depreciated at the rate of:

$$\frac{£20,000}{10 \text{ years}} = £2,000 \text{ per annum}$$

(b)   A fixed asset costing £60,000 has an estimated life of five years and a residual value of £7,000. The annual depreciation charge using the straight line method would be calculated as follows.

$$\frac{£(60,000 - 7,000)}{5 \text{ years}} = £10,600 \text{ per annum}$$

The net book value of the fixed asset would reduce each year as follows.

	After 1 year £	*After 2 years* £	*After 3 years* £	*After 4 years* £	*After 5 years* £
Cost of the asset	60,000	60,000	60,000	60,000	60,000
Accumulated depreciation	10,600	21,200	31,800	42,400	53,000
Net book value	49,400	38,800	28,200	17,600	7,000*

* ie its estimated residual value.

2.16   Since the depreciation charge per annum is the same amount every year with the straight line method, it is often convenient to state that depreciation is charged at the rate of x per cent per annum on the cost of the asset. In the example in Paragraph 2.15(a) above, the depreciation charge per annum is 10% of cost (ie 10% of £20,000 = £2,000).

2.17   The straight line method of depreciation is a fair allocation of the total depreciable amount between the different accounting periods, provided that it is reasonable to assume that the business enjoys *equal benefits* from the use of the asset in every period throughout its life.

The reducing balance method

2.18   The reducing balance method of depreciation calculates the annual depreciation charge as a *fixed percentage* of the net book value of the asset, as at the end of the previous accounting period.

2.19   Suppose that a business purchases a fixed asset at a cost of £10,000. Its expected useful life is three years and its estimated residual value is £2,160. The business wishes to use the reducing balance method to depreciate the asset, and calculates that the rate of depreciation should be 40% of the reducing (net book) value of the asset. (The method of deciding that 40% is a suitable percentage is a problem of mathematics and is not described here.)

The total depreciable amount is £(10,000 – 2,160) = £7,840.

The depreciation charge per annum and the net book value of the asset as at the end of each year will be as follows.

	£	Accumulated depreciation £
Asset at cost	10,000	
Depreciation in year 1 (40%)	4,000	4,000
Net book value at end of year	6,000	
Depreciation in year 2		
(40% of reducing balance)	2,400	6,400 (4,000 + 2,400)
Net book value at end of year	3,600	
Depreciation in year 3 (40%)	1,440	7,840 (6,400 + 1,440)
Net book value at end of year	2,160	

2.20 You should be able to see that with the reducing balance method, the annual charge for depreciation is higher in the earlier years of the asset's life, and lower in the later years. In the example above, the annual charges for years 1, 2 and 3 are £4,000, £2,400 and £1,440 respectively.

2.21 The reducing balance method might be used when it is considered fair to allocate a *greater proportion* of the total depreciable amount to the earlier years and a lower amount in the later years, on the assumption that the benefits obtained by the business from using the asset decline over time.

Which method of depreciation should be used?

2.22 A business is faced with a choice between the various methods of depreciation for its different types of fixed assets. A different method can be used for each type of asset, such as buildings, machinery, motor vehicles and so on. The method chosen must, however, be fair in allocating the charges between different accounting periods.

2.23 The following needs to be taken into consideration when selecting a method of depreciation.

(a) The method should allocate costs in proportion to the *benefits* (revenues or profits) earned during each accounting period by the asset. These profits almost certainly cannot be calculated exactly, but the business should be able to decide whether:

(i) the asset provides greater benefits in the earlier years of its life, in which case the reducing balance method would be suitable; or

(ii) the asset provides equal benefits to each period throughout its life, in which case the straight line method would be suitable.

(b) The method of depreciation used by a business for any fixed asset should be the same as the method used for *similar assets*.

(c) The method used should be one which is *easy to apply* in practice. There is no point in creating unnecessary complications.

The straight line method is by far the most common method used in practice. It is easy to use and it is generally fair to assume that all periods benefit more or less equally from the use of a fixed asset throughout its useful life.

Assets acquired in the middle of an accounting period

2.24 A business will purchase new fixed assets at any time during the course of an accounting period, and so it might seem fair to charge an amount for depreciation in the period when the purchase occurs which reflects the limited amount of use the business has had from the asset in that period.

Example: Assets acquired during an accounting period

2.25 Suppose that a business which has an accounting year which runs from 1 January to 31 December purchases a new fixed asset on 1 April 19X1, at a cost of £24,000. The expected life of the asset is four years, and its residual value is nil.

What should be the depreciation charge for 19X1?

Solution: Assets acquired during an accounting period

2.26 The annual depreciation charge will be $\dfrac{24,000}{4 \text{ years}}$ = £6,000 per annum.

However, since the asset was acquired on 1 April 19X1, the business has only benefited from the use of the asset for nine months instead of a full 12 months. It would therefore seem fair to charge nine months' depreciation in 19X1 as follows.

$^9/_{12} \times £6,000 = £4,500$

2.27 If you are given a purchase date of a fixed asset which is in the middle of an accounting period, you should generally assume that depreciation should be calculated in this way, as a 'part-year' amount. However, you should be aware that in practice, many businesses ignore the niceties of part-year depreciation, and charge a full year's depreciation on fixed assets in the year of their purchase, regardless of the time of year they were acquired.

Recording depreciation in the accounts

2.28 We must now consider how to record depreciation in the ledger accounts. There are two basic aspects of the provision for depreciation to remember.

(a) A *depreciation charge* is made in the profit and loss account of each accounting period for every depreciable fixed asset.

(b) The total *accumulated depreciation* on a fixed asset builds up as the asset gets older. Unlike a provision for doubtful debts, therefore, the total provision for depreciation is always getting larger, until the fixed asset is fully depreciated.

2.29 The ledger accounting period entries for the provision for depreciation are as follows.

(a) There is a provision for depreciation account for each separate category of fixed assets.

(b) The depreciation charge for an accounting period is an additional provision for depreciation and is accounted for as follows.

DEBIT   Depreciation expense (in the P & L account)
CREDIT   Provision for depreciation account

(c) The balance on the provision for depreciation account is the total accumulated depreciation. This is always a credit balance brought forward in the ledger account for depreciation.

(d) The fixed asset accounts are unaffected by depreciation. Fixed assets are recorded in these accounts at cost.

(e) In the balance sheet of the business, the total balance on the provision for depreciation account (ie accumulated depreciation) is set against the value of fixed asset accounts (ie fixed assets at cost) to derive the net book value of the fixed assets.

Example: Ledger entries for depreciation (1)

2.30 Brian Box set up his own computer software business on 1 March 19X6. He purchased a computer system on credit from a manufacturer, at a cost of £16,000. The system has an expected life of three years and a residual value of £2,500. Using the straight line method of depreciation, the fixed asset account, provision for depreciation account and profit and loss account (extract) and balance sheet (extract) would be as follows, for each of the next three years, 28 February 19X7, 19X8 and 19X9.

FIXED ASSET: COMPUTER EQUIPMENT

	Date		£	Date		£
(a)	1 Mar 19X6	Creditor	16,000	28 Feb 19X7	Balance c/d	16,000
(b)	1 Mar 19X7	Balance b/d	16,000	28 Feb 19X8	Balance c/d	16,000
(c)	1 Mar 19X8	Balance b/d	16,000	28 Feb 19X9	Balance c/d	16,000
(d)	1 Mar 19X9	Balance b/d	16,000			

In theory, the fixed asset has now lasted out its expected useful life. However, until it is sold off or scrapped, the asset will still appear in the balance sheet at cost, less accumulated depreciation, and it should remain in the ledger account for computer equipment until it is eventually disposed of.

PROVISION FOR DEPRECIATION

	Date		£	Date		£
(a)	28 Feb 19X7	Balance c/d	4,500	28 Feb 19X7	Dep'n expense	4,500
(b)	28 Feb 19X8	Balance c/d	9,000	1 Mar 19X7	Balance b/d	4,500
				28 Feb 19X8	Dep'n expense	4,500
			9,000			9,000
(c)	28 Feb 19X9	Balance c/d	13,500	1 Mar 19X8	Balance b/d	9,000
				28 Feb 19X9	Dep'n expense	4,500
			13,500			13,500
				1 Mar 19X9	Balance b/d	13,500

The annual depreciation charge is $\dfrac{£(16,000 - 2,500)}{3 \text{ years}} = £4,500$

At the end of three years, the asset is fully depreciated down to its residual value of £2,500. If it continues to be used by Brian Box, it will not be depreciated any further (unless its estimated residual value is reduced).

DEPRECIATION EXPENSE ACCOUNT (EXTRACT)

	Date		£
(a)	28 Feb 19X7	Provision for depreciation	4,500
(b)	28 Feb 19X8	Provision for depreciation	4,500
(c)	28 Feb 19X9	Provision for depreciation	4,500

BALANCE SHEET (EXTRACT) AS AT 28 FEBRUARY

	19X7(a) £	19X8(b) £	19X9(c) £
Computer equipment at cost	16,000	16,000	16,000
Less accumulated depreciation	4,500	9,000	13,500
Net book value	11,500	7,000	2,500

Example: Ledger entries for depreciation (2)

2.31 Brian Box prospers in his computer software business, and before long he purchases a car for himself, and later for his chief assistant Bill Ockhead. Relevant data is as follows.

	Date of purchase	Cost	Estimated life	Estimated residual value
Brian Box car	1 June 19X6	£20,000	3 years	£2,000
Bill Ockhead car	1 June 19X7	£8,000	3 years	£2,000

The straight line method of depreciation is to be used.

Task

Prepare the motor vehicles account and provision for depreciation of motor vehicle account for the years to 28 February 19X7 and 19X8. (You should allow for the part-year's use of a car in computing the annual charge for depreciation.) Calculate the net book value of the motor vehicles as at 28 February 19X8.

Solution: Ledger entries for depreciation

2.32 *Workings*

(1) *Brian Box car*   Annual depreciation $\dfrac{£(20,000 - 2,000)}{3 \text{ years}}$ = £6,000pa

Depreciation	Monthly depreciation	£500
	1 June 19X6 to 28 February 19X7 (9 months)	£4,500
	1 March 19X7 to 28 February 19X8	£6,000

(2) *Bill Ockhead car*   Annual depreciation $\dfrac{£(8,000 - 2,000)}{3 \text{ years}}$ = £2,000pa

Depreciation 1 June 19X7 to 28 February 19X8 (9 months)   £1,500

MOTOR VEHICLES

Date		£	Date		£
1 June 19X6	Creditor (or cash) (car purchase)	20,000	28 Feb 19X7	Balance c/d	20,000
1 March 19X7	Balance b/d	20,000			
1 June 19X7	Creditors (or cash) (car purchase)	8,000	28 Feb 19X8	Balance c/d	28,000
		28,000			28,000
1 Mar 19X8	Balance b/d	28,000			

PROVISION FOR DEPRECIATION OF MOTOR VEHICLES

Date		£	Date		£
28 Feb 19X7	Balance c/d	4,500	28 Feb 19X7	Dep'n expense	4,500
			1 Mar 19X7	Balance b/d	4,500
28 Feb 19X8	Balance c/d	12,000	28 Feb 19X8	Dep'n expense £(6,000+1,500)	7,500
		12,000			12,000
			1 Mar 19X8	Balance b/d	12,000

BALANCE SHEET (WORKINGS) AS AT 28 FEBRUARY 19X8

	Brian Box car		Bill Ockhead car		Total
	£	£	£	£	£
Asset at cost		20,000		8,000	28,000
Accumulated depreciation Year to:					
28 Feb 19X7	4,500		-		
28 Feb 19×	6,000		1,500		
		10,500		1,500	12,000
Net book value		9,500		6,500	16,000

Change in the useful economic life of an asset

2.33 SSAP 12 states that the useful economic life of an asset should be reviewed regularly. If the estimate has to be revised, the depreciation charge must be adjusted accordingly.

2.34   Consider for example a fixed asset costing £10,000 in 19X1 which was originally estimated to last 10 years, depreciation to be charged using the straight line method. The depreciation charge would be £1,000 pa.

2.35   Suppose, however, that at the beginning of 19X7 it was estimated that the asset would last only for another two years instead of four. Using the straight line method the residual value would have to be written off over 2 years, resulting in a charge of 4,000/2, ie £2,000 pa.

3   PURCHASE AND SALE OF FIXED ASSETS
Centrally assessed 6/94, 12/94, 12/95, 6/96, 12/96

Posting the ledger from a book of prime entry

3.1   So far we have discussed entries for capital transactions in asset accounts, depreciation accounts and provision accounts without any mention of the fact that they are first recorded in a book of prime entry.

3.2   The book of prime entry in which credit purchases and sales of fixed assets and depreciation transfers are generally first recorded is the *journal*. Cash transactions are recorded in the cash book. You will have come across the journal in your earlier studies and we discussed it again in Chapter 1. It is used to record those transactions which take place only infrequently. Purchases and sales of fixed assets do not normally take place very often and depreciation transfers will only take place at the end of an accounting period.

Example of journal entries for credit purchase and sale of fixed assets

3.3   An example of journal entries relating to purchase and sale of fixed assets on credit is shown below. Do not worry if you do not understand some of the entries relating to the sale of fixed assets. These will be considered in Paragraph 3.6 below. The folio references indicate the appropriate ledger accounts.

JOURNAL

Page 51

Date	Details	Folio Ref	£	£
12 June	Motor vehicles a/c Van Gogh Ltd Being purchase of delivery van reg. E298 PTO per invoice no. ED/142	NLM2 SLV6	14,500	14,500
13 June	Furniture a/c Sofa Miredo Being purchase of sofa for reception invoice no. LA/TI123	NLF1 BLS12	1,000	1,000
14 June	Sid's Tool Works Plant disposal a/c Being part exchange value of machine no. 8 per agreement and invoice XY/149	SLP2 NLD3	575	575
14 June	Plant disposal a/c Plant a/c Being written down value of machine 8 part exchanged transferred to plant disposal account	NLD3 NLP2	500	500
14 June	Plant disposal a/c Profit and Loss a/c Being profit on part exchange of machine no. 8	NLD3 PL1	75	75

Example of journal entries for year end depreciation transfer

3.4 Suppose depreciation on motor vehicles which cost £100,000 is to be calculated at 20% on cost for the year ended 30 September. The journal entries required are shown below.

				£	£
JOURNAL					**Page 142**
Date	Details	Folio Ref		£	£
30 Sept	Motor vehicles depreciation a/c	NLD2		20,000	
	Motor vehicles provision for depreciation	NLP3			20,000
	Being year-end provision for depreciation				

Accounting for the disposal of fixed assets

3.5 Eventually, most tangible fixed assets are disposed of. They might be disposed of as soon as their estimated useful life is finished, or they might be disposed of either before then or later. A profit on disposal is an item of 'other income' in the profit and loss account, and a loss on disposal is an item of expense in the profit and loss account.

3.6 It is customary in ledger accounting to record the disposal of fixed assets in a *disposal of fixed assets account*. If you look at the journals above you will see these entries being posted.

(a) The profit or loss on disposal is the difference between:

    (i)   the sale price of the asset (if any); and
    (ii)   the net book value of the asset at the time of sale.

(b) The relevant items which must appear in the disposal of fixed assets account are as follows.

    (i)   The original value of the asset at cost
    (ii)   The accumulated depreciation up to the date of sale
    (iii) The sale price of the asset

(c) The ledger accounting entries are as follows.

    (i)   DEBIT   Disposal of fixed asset account
              CREDIT   Fixed asset account

             with the cost of the asset disposed of.

    (ii)   DEBIT   Provision for depreciation account
              CREDIT   Disposal of fixed asset account

             with the accumulated depreciation on the asset as at the date of sale.

    (iii) DEBIT   Debtor account or cash book
              CREDIT   Disposal of fixed asset account

             with the sale price of the asset. The sale is therefore not recorded in a sales account, but in the disposal of fixed asset account.

(iv)   The balance on the disposal account is the profit or loss on disposal and the corresponding double entry is recorded in the profit and loss account.

Example: Ledger entries for the disposal of fixed assets

3.7   A business has £110,000 worth of machinery at cost. Its policy is to make a provision for depreciation at 20% per annum straight line. The total provision now stands at £70,000. The business now sells for £19,000 a machine which it purchased exactly two years ago for £30,000.

Show the relevant ledger entries.

Solution: Ledger entries for the disposal of fixed assets

3.8

PLANT AND MACHINERY ACCOUNT

	£		£
Balance b/d	110,000	Plant disposals account	30,000
		Balance c/d	80,000
	110,000		110,000
Balance b/d	80,000		

PLANT AND MACHINERY DEPRECIATION PROVISION

	£		£
Plant disposals (20% of £30,000 for 2 years)	12,000	Balance b/d	70,000
Balance c/d	58,000		
	70,000		70,000
		Balance b/d	58,000

PLANT DISPOSALS

	£		£
Plant and machinery account	30,000	Depreciation provision	12,000
P&L a/c (profit on sale)	1,000	Cash	19,000
	31,000		31,000

Check

	£
Asset at cost	30,000
Accumulated depreciation at time of sale	12,000
Net book value at time of sale	18,000
Sale price	19,000
Profit on sale	1,000

Example continued

3.9   Taking the example in Paragraph 3.7, assume that, instead of the machine being sold for £19,000, it was exchanged for a new machine costing £60,000, a credit of £19,000 being received upon exchange. In other words, £19,000 is the trade-in price of the old machine.

Solution continued

3.10

PLANT AND MACHINERY ACCOUNT

	£		£
Balance b/d	110,000	Plant disposal	30,000
Cash £(60,000 – 19,000)	41,000	Balance c/d	140,000
Plant disposals	19,000		
	170,000		170,000
Balance b/d	140,000		

Notes

(1) The new asset is recorded in the fixed asset account at cost £(41,000 + 19,000) = £60,000.

(2) The other two accounts, plant and machinery depreciation provision and plant disposals, will be the same as in Paragraph 3.8 above.

Further example: Ledger entries for the disposal of fixed assets

3.11 A business purchased two widget-making machines on 1 January 19X5 at a cost of £15,000 each. Each had an estimated life of five years and a nil residual value. The straight line method of depreciation is used.

Owing to an unforeseen slump in market demand for widgets, the business decided to reduce its output of widgets, and switch to making other products instead. On 31 March 19X7, one widget-making machine was sold (on credit) to a buyer for £8,000. Later in the year, however, it was decided to abandon production of widgets altogether, and the second machine was sold on 1 December 19X7 for £2,500 cash.

Task

Prepare the machinery account, provision for depreciation of machinery account and disposal of machinery account for the accounting year to 31 December 19X7.

Solution: Ledger entries for the disposal of fixed assets

3.12 *Workings*

(1) At 1 January 19X7, accumulated depreciation on the machines will be:

$$2 \text{ machines} \times 2 \text{ years} \times \frac{£15,000}{5} = £12,000, \text{ or } £6,000 \text{ per machine}$$

(2) Monthly depreciation is $\frac{£3,000}{12} = £250$ per machine per month

(3) The machines are disposed of in 19X7.

(i) *On 31 March:* after three months of the year

Depreciation for the year on the machine = 3 months × £250 = £750

(ii) *On 1 December:* after 11 months of the year

Depreciation for the year on the machine = 11 months × £250 = £2,750

MACHINERY ACCOUNT

Date		£	Date		£
19X7			19X7		
1 Jan	Balance b/f	30,000	31 Mar	Disposal of machinery account	15,000
			1 Dec	Disposal of machinery account	15,000
		30,000			30,000

PROVISION FOR DEPRECIATION OF MACHINERY

Date		£	Date		£
19X7			19X7		
31 Mar	Disposal of machinery account*	6,750	1 Jan	Balance b/f	12,000
1 Dec	Disposal of machinery account**	8,750	31 Dec	P & L account***	3,500
		15,500			15,500

*Depreciation at date of disposal = £6,000 + £750
**Depreciation at date of disposal = £6,000 + £2,750
***Depreciation charge for the year = £750 + £2,750

DISPOSAL OF MACHINERY

Date 19X7		£	Date 19X7		£
31 Mar	Machinery account	15,000	31 Mar	Debtor account (sale price)	8,000
			31 Mar	Provision for depreciation	6,750
1 Dec	Machinery account	15,000	1 Dec	Cash (sale price)	2,500
			1 Dec	Provision for depreciation	8,750
			31 Dec	P & L account (loss on disposal)	4,000
		30,000			30,000

You should be able to calculate that there was a loss on the first disposal of £250, and on the second disposal a loss of £3,750, giving a total loss of £4,000.

Labour costs in the installation of fixed assets

3.13 When a business uses its own work force to install some fixed assets, the cost of the labour may be added to the cost of the fixed asset. The ledger accounting entries are simply:

DEBIT   Fixed asset account
CREDIT   Wages/salaries account

with the labour cost of the installation.

4   THE FIXED ASSETS REGISTER

4.1 Capital transactions represent considerable sums spent by a company. There could be many valuable fixed assets kept in various departments or on factory floors. Occasionally some of these would be scrapped or sold off and replaced by new ones. With such a large amount of investment capital tied up in fixed assets, *tight control* of the details concerning each fixed asset is required. As mentioned above, the journal is used as a book of prime entry to record the purchase and sale of fixed assets, but this is not sufficient to record and control what happens to them.

4.2 Nearly all but the smallest organisations keep a *fixed assets register*. This is a listing of all fixed assets owned by the organisation, broken down perhaps by department, location or asset type.

4.3 A fixed assets register is kept mainly for internal purposes. It is not part of the double entry system and does not record rights over or obligations towards third parties but shows an organisation's investment in capital equipment. A fixed asset register is also part of the *internal control* system. This is discussed further in Section 5 below. Fixed assets registers or ledgers are sometimes called *real accounts*, to distinguish them from *impersonal accounts* such as 'rent' in the nominal ledger and *personal accounts* such as 'A Detta' in the sales ledger. They tend to include very few transactions and for this reason they are separated from those accounts that are more heavily used.

Data kept in a fixed assets register

4.4 Details held about each fixed asset *might* include the following.

(a) The organisation's internal reference number (for physical identification purposes)
(b) Manufacturer's serial number (for maintenance purposes)
(c) Description of asset
(d) Location of asset
(e) Insurance details (sometimes)
(f) Department which 'owns' asset

4.5 However, the most important details from an accounting point of view will be as follows.

  (a) Purchase date (for calculation of depreciation)
  (b) Cost
  (c) Depreciation method and estimated useful life (for calculation of depreciation)
  (d) Accumulated depreciation brought forward and carried forward
  (e) Disposal proceeds
  (f) Profit/loss on disposal

4.6 The main events giving rise to entries in a fixed asset register or 'inputs' in the case of a computerised one, would be the following.

  (a) Purchase of an asset
  (b) Sale of an asset
  (c) Loss or destruction of an asset
  (d) Transfer of assets between departments
  (e) Revision of estimated useful life of an asset
  (f) Scrapping of an asset

4.7 'Outputs' from a fixed assets register would be made:

  (a) to enable reconciliations to be made to the nominal ledger;
  (b) to enable depreciation charges to be posted to the nominal ledger; and
  (c) for physical verification/audit purposes.

Layout of fixed assets register

4.8 The layout of a fixed assets register and the degree of detail included will depend on the organisation in question. Some may have an individual page devoted to each type of fixed asset. Others may have columns across the page for various headings and list the assets in an organised way, for example by department or by the type of asset it is. Below is a fairly typical layout from a fixed assets register which is maintained *manually*.

Date of purchase	Invoice number	Ref	Item	Cost	Accum'd dep'n b/f	Dep'n expense	Accum'd dep'n c/f	Date of disposal	Disposal proceeds	(Loss)/ gain

4.9 Most fixed assets registers will be *computerised*. Here is an extract from a fixed asset register showing one item as it might appear when the details are printed out.

FASSET HOLDINGS PLC

Asset Code: 938   Next depreciation: 539.36

A	Description:	1 × Seisha Laser printer YCA40809 office publisher
B	Date of purchase:	25/05/X4
C	Cost:	1618.25
D	Accumulated depreciation:	584.35
E	Depreciation %:	33.33%
F	Depreciation type:	straight line
G	Date of disposal:	NOT SET
H	Sale proceeds:	0.00
I	Accumulated depreciation amount:	55Q O/EQPT DEP CHARGE
J	Depreciation expense account:	34F DEPN O/EQPT
K	Depreciation period:	standard
L	Comments:	Electronic office
M	Residual value:	0.00
N	Cost account:	65C O/E ADDITIONS

---

5   AUTHORISATION AND CONTROL

Authorisation

5.1   Capital expenditure over a certain amount must normally be authorised by directors of a company and major projects will be noted in the minutes of board meetings. Generally, a document called a *capital expenditure authorisation form* (or some similar name) is used.

5.2   The capital expenditure authorisation form should show the prior authority for capital expenditure and indicate the approved method of funding, ie outright purchase or lease. Below is an example of a capital expenditure authorisation form.

CAPITAL EXPENDITURE
AUTHORISATION FORM

Company/Division ....

Description of item and reason for purchase ....

....

....

Supplier ....

Cost ....

Was this the cheapest quote obtained (if not state reason)? ....

....

....

Authorised by: ....

Counter-authorised (if over £1,000) by: ....

Purchase/lease* ....

Terms of lease ....

....

PLEASE RETURN TO PENNY WISE, FINANCIAL CONTROLLER

* delete as applicable

5.3   A *disposal* (ie sale or scrapping of an asset) over a certain amount must also be authorised. Below is an asset disposal authorisation form. You should note that the form contains a space to insert the reason for disposal. This will generally be that the asset has become obsolete or worn out but it could be that the asset was not present at the last physical count, in which case the 'sale proceeds' would obviously be nil.

ASSET DISPOSAL

AUTHORISATION FORM

Company/Division ....

Description and location of asset ....

....

....

Date of purchase ....

Date of disposal ....

Original cost ....

Accumulated depreciation ....

Net book value ....

Sale/scrap proceeds ....

Profit/loss to profit and loss account ....

Reason for disposal ....

....

....

Authorised by: ....

Counter-authorised (if original cost over £1,000) by: ....

PLEASE RETURN TO PENNY WISE, FINANCIAL CONTROLLER

Control

5.4   It is important, both from the point of view of external reporting (ie the audit) and for internal purposes, that there are *controls* over fixed assets. The fixed assets register has already been mentioned. Two further points should be made in this context.

(a)   The fixed assets register might not reconcile with the nominal ledger.

(b)   The fixed assets register might not reconcile with the physical presence of capital items.

Each of these will be examined in turn.

The fixed assets register and the nominal ledger

5.5   Generally, the fixed assets register is not integrated with the nominal ledger. If you look at our example of a fixed assets register in Paragraph 4.8 above, you will see that the entry lists the nominal ledger accounts (cost account, accumulated depreciation account and depreciation expense account) to which the relevant amounts must be posted and also contains other details not required in those nominal accounts. In other words, the fixed assets register is not part of the double entry and is there for memorandum and control purposes.

5.6   The fixed asset register must therefore be *reconciled* to the nominal ledger to make sure that all additions, disposals and depreciation provisions and charges have been posted. For example, the total of all the 'cost' figures in the fixed assets register for motor vehicles should equal the balance on the 'motor vehicles cost' account in the nominal ledger, and the same goes for accumulated depreciation.

5.7 If an asset is sold off, this should be properly authorised, the asset released, the register completed and the necessary entries made in the journal and ledger accounts.

5.8 If discrepancies arise between the register and the nominal ledger, these must be investigated. It could be, for example, that there is a delay in sending the appropriate authorisation form where an asset has been disposed of.

The fixed assets register and the fixed assets

5.9 It is possible that the fixed assets register may not reconcile with the fixed assets actually present. This may be for the following reasons.

(a) An asset has been *stolen* and this has not been noticed or not recorded.

(b) A fixed asset may have become *obsolete* or *damaged* and needs to be written down but the appropriate entries have not been made.

(c) New assets have been *purchased* but not yet recorded in the register because the register has not been kept up to date.

(d) *Errors* have been made in entering details in the register.

5.10 It is important therefore that the company:

(a) physically inspects all the items in the fixed assets register; and
(b) keeps the fixed assets register up to date.

The nature of the inspection will obviously vary between organisations. A large company might carry out a fixed asset inspection of, for example, 25% of assets by value each year, aiming to cover all categories every four years. A small company might be able to inspect all its fixed assets each day, although this 'inspection' will probably not be formally recorded.

Dealing with discrepancies

5.11 As mentioned in Paragraph 5.9 above, some assets may require an adjustment in their expected life due to excessive wear and tear. The proper authority to change any estimations to the life of an asset must have the correct authorisation, and the information should be communicated to the accounts department who will need to make adjustments in the journal, the register and the ledger.

5.12 When discrepancies are discovered, the appropriate action must be taken. It may be possible to resolve the discrepancy by updating the fixed assets register and/or nominal ledger to reflect the new position. It may not be possible for the person who discovers the discrepancy to resolve it himself. For example, if a fixed asset has to be revalued downwards due to wear and tear or obsolescence, he may have to refer the matter to his superior who has more experience and judgement in such matters.

Computer-based asset management systems

5.13 Very large companies can now use computer-based asset management systems which work on *barcodes*, ie all assets have a barcode affixed on purchase and hand-held barcode readers can be used to check assets to the register automatically. This makes the management of assets much easier, but it is expensive to install. Barcodes do combat theft, however, and the subsequent savings for large companies can be substantial.

Key points in this chapter

- *Capital expenditure* results in the acquisition of fixed assets or an improvement in their earning capacity. *Revenue expenditure* is expenditure which is incurred for the purpose of the trade of the business or to maintain the existing earning capacity of fixed assets.

- Only *material* items should be capitalised.

- Since a fixed asset has a cost and a limited useful life and its value eventually declines, it follows that a charge should be made in the trading, profit and loss account to reflect the use that is made of the asset by the business. This charge is called *depreciation*.

- The two most common *methods* of depreciation are the straight line method and the reducing balance method.

- The *accounting entries* to record depreciation are:

  DEBIT   Depreciation expense account (in the P & L)
  CREDIT   Provision for depreciation account

- The book of prime entry from which postings are made relating to purchases, sales and depreciation of fixed assets is the *journal*.

- The *profit or loss on disposal* of fixed assets is the difference between the sale price of the asset and the net book value of the asset at the time of sale.

- Most organisations keep a *fixed assets register*. This is a listing of all fixed assets owned by the organisation broken down perhaps by department, location or asset type. This must be kept up to date.

- *Discrepancies* between the fixed assets register and the actual fixed assets present and between the fixed assets register and the nominal ledger must be investigated and either resolved or referred to the appropriate person.

- Additions and disposals over a certain amount must be *authorised* on a capital expenditure authorisation form and a disposal authorisation form respectively.

For practice on the points covered in this chapter you should now attempt the Practice Exercises in Session 4 of the Financial Accounting Workbook

Part C
Recording income and expenditure

5 Final accounts and the accounting system

This chapter covers the following topics.

1   Introduction to final accounts

2   Management accounts

3   The accounting system

4   Classifying income and expenditure

5   SSAP 5 Accounting for value added tax

6   SSAP 13 Accounting for research and development

7   SSAP 21 Accounting for leases and hire purchase contracts

---

1 INTRODUCTION TO FINAL ACCOUNTS

Starting at the end

1.1 We are starting our examination of the preparation of financial accounts at the end of the process: the final accounts. You will thus be able to keep in mind what we are trying to achieve as we proceed through each stage of the preparation process. You have already looked at basic accounting in your earlier studies, including the accounting system, ledger accounting and the concept of double entry bookkeeping. In this text we will develop and extend this basic knowledge, building up your skills in bookkeeping and accounts preparation.

1.2 As well as looking at a set of final accounts, we will also look at some of the rules which must be used when preparing company accounts. These rules are contained in Statements of Standard Accounting Practice (SSAPs) and Financial Reporting Standards (FRSs) which, as we have seen, are formulated and issued by the Accounting Standards Board. You will find a full description of the nature and purpose of SSAPs and FRSs in Chapter 3 of this Tutorial Text. In the following chapters, however, we will look only at those SSAPs and FRSs which directly affect the preparation of accounts.

Why prepare accounts?

1.3 There are many different reasons for preparing accounts, but those given below are the main ones.

(a) All limited companies are obliged by law to prepare accounts (usually yearly) in specific formats laid out in the Companies Act 1985 (see Paragraph 1.5 below). These accounts form part of the company report which must be sent to all shareholders and filed at Companies House with the Registrar of Companies.

(b) The managers of a business, whether it is a limited company or not, will want to know how well (or badly) the business is doing, and particularly whether it is making a profit. Regular *management accounts* (often monthly) will help the managers control and guide the business.

(c) In some businesses the accounts are used to calculate some important numbers, such as the share of profit due to each partner or the bonus due to the directors or managers.

(d) Accounts must be prepared as a basis for the calculation of the tax due on any profits of the business.

1.4 Whatever the primary reason is for the preparation of accounts, generally all items are recorded in the same way, although the presentation of the information in the final accounts may differ. This chapter is concerned with how items of income and expenditure are recorded and classified, but first we will look at two examples of sets of accounts, company accounts and management accounts.

Company accounts

1.5 The following set of accounts is a slightly simplified example of one of the formats specified in the Companies Act 1985 ('CA 1985') for the accounts of limited companies. Although other alternative formats specified in CA 1985 may alternatively be used, the format below is the most commonly used and accepted in practice.

KROOK LIMITED
BALANCE SHEET AS AT 31 DECEMBER 19X2

	£	£
Fixed assets		
Tangible assets	7,562	
Intangible assets	11,000	
		18,562
Current assets		
Stock	55,317	
Debtors	67,109	
Cash	11,425	
	133,851	
Creditors: amounts falling due		
within one year (see Note)	64,217	
Net current assets		69,634
		88,196
Creditors: amounts falling due		
after one year		
Debenture loans		9,296
		78,900
Capital and reserves		
Called up share capital		
£1 ordinary shares		45,000
Profit and loss account		33,900
		78,900

Note. This amount will consist of trade creditors, bank overdrafts, tax payable, accruals and dividends payable, all due within a year.

KROOK LIMITED
PROFIT AND LOSS ACCOUNT FOR THE YEAR ENDED 31 DECEMBER 19X2

	£
Turnover	337,500
Cost of sales	242,640
Gross profit	94,860
Distribution costs	55,985
Administration expenses	15,632
Operating profit	23,243
Interest payable	855
Profit on ordinary activities before tax	22,388
Taxation	8,936
Profit on ordinary activities after tax	13,452
Dividends	6,237
Retained profits for the year	7,215
Retained profit brought forward	26,685
Retained profit carried forward	33,900

1.6 You will probably be more familiar with the accounts of an unincorporated business from your earlier studies, but the accounts of limited companies follow most of the same principles. Some of the items which are unfamiliar will be explained as we proceed.

1.7 The balance sheet and profit and loss account shown above represent the basis of the published accounts of a limited company. Other information, by way of statements and notes, must be shown according to company law and accounting standards. At the moment, however, we are only concerned with the production of the basic information required for the balance sheet and the profit and loss account. Let us consider for the moment what the balance sheet and profit and loss account actually represent.

Balance sheet

1.8 The balance sheet is a picture of all the assets owned by a business and all the liabilities owed by a business at a particular date and it shows the financial state of the business. You should remember from your earlier studies on the accounting equation that the sum of the assets will always equal the sum of the liabilities. You should be familiar with all the components of the balance sheet, except perhaps *share capital*. This is simply the equivalent of the proprietor's capital. The shares are denominated in units of 25 pence, 50 pence, £1 or whatever amount is appropriate. The 'face value' of the shares is called their *nominal value*. Shares are issued by the company when it is formed, and at various times in the future if further capital is required. The profit and loss account balance shown here is the accumulated profits and losses of the company since incorporation.

Profit and loss account

1.9   The profit and loss account is a record of income generated and expenditure incurred over a given period; for a limited company this will usually be one year, commencing from the date of the previous year's accounts. The profit and loss account shows whether the business has succeeded in generating more income than expenditure (a profit) or vice versa (a loss). Organisations which are not run for profit (such as charities) produce a similar statement called an *income and expenditure account* which shows the surplus of income over expenditure (or deficit where expenditure exceeds income).

1.10   As we saw earlier, the profit and loss account can be divided into two parts.

(a)   The *trading account* shows the gross profit for the accounting period. Gross profit is the difference between:

(i)   the value of sales (excluding VAT); and

(ii)   the purchase cost or production cost of the goods sold (which we will consider later when we look at stock valuation).

(b)   The *profit and loss account* shows the net profit of the business, which is:

(i)   the gross profit;

(ii)   *plus* any other income from sources other than the sale of goods (such as interest earned on bank deposits and profits from selling off unwanted fixed assets);

(iii) *less* any other expenses of the business which are not included in the cost of goods sold, generally administration, distribution and selling expenses.

1.11   Note that, in the trading account, purchases are not the same as the cost of goods sold during the period, because:

(a)   items purchased during the period might be held in stock at the end of the period; and

(b)   items held in stock at the start of the period might be sold in the current period.

We will examine the cost of goods sold in Chapter 7.

Accounting concepts

1.12   Remember that accounts are prepared under the four basic accounting concepts contained in SSAP 2 *Disclosure of accounting policies,* explained in detail in Chapter 2 of this Tutorial Text. We will recap on the four concepts briefly here.

(a)   The *accruals or matching concept* states that revenues and costs are accrued (that is, recognised as they are earned or incurred, not as money is received or paid), matched with one another as far as their relationship can be established or justifiably assumed, and dealt with in the profit and loss account for the period to which they relate. We will return to this concept later as it is fundamental to the mechanics of preparing accounts.

(b)   The *consistency concept* states that, in preparing accounts, consistency should be observed in two respects.

(i)   Similar items within a single set of accounts should be given similar accounting treatment.

(ii) The same treatment should be applied from one period to another in accounting for similar items.

(c) The *going concern concept* implies that the business will continue in operational existence for the foreseeable future, and that there is no intention to put the company into liquidation or to make drastic cutbacks to the scale of operations. The main significance of the going concern concept is that the assets of the business should not be valued at their 'break up' value, which is the amount that they would sell for if the business were broken up and they were sold off piecemeal.

(d) Under the *prudence concept,* revenues and profits are not anticipated, but are included in the profit and loss account only when realised in the form either of cash (or of other assets which will definitely be realised in cash soon). Provision is made for all known expenses or losses whether the amount of these is known with certainty or a best estimate must be used in the light of the information available. In some circumstances the prudence concept and accruals concept will come into conflict; where this happens, the prudence concept shall prevail.

1.13 The descriptions given here are taken from SSAP 2 and you should remember them as we proceed through the stages of preparing accounts. One other concept is introduced by the Companies Act 1985 (which also recognises the other four) and that is the *separate valuation principle*. This states that each component item of the asset or liability in question must be valued separately. These separate valuations must then be added together to arrive at the balance sheet figure. This will be explained in greater detail when we look at stock valuation in Chapter 7.

2 MANAGEMENT ACCOUNTS

2.1 We mentioned above that the managers of a business will want to see accounts more frequently than once a year, so that they can see how well the business is doing. Monthly or quarterly information will allow the managers to gauge the success of their decisions, or to change strategy when things have not gone according to plan. They will therefore often have a budget, which shows the expected result for the period, with which to compare the actual results. The budget will usually be formulated on a yearly basis, but it may be adjusted to take account of results to date in the year.

2.2 It is not within the scope of Unit 5 to prepare budgets or management accounts. However, you should be aware of the different uses which may be made of accounting information. We have already looked at the format of published company accounts. Here is an example of what a set of management accounts might look like.

June management accounts

	Month(a) £'000	Budget(b) £'000	YTD(c) £'000	Budget for year Year(d) £'000	Plan(e) £'000
Sales	95	100	1,000	2,400	2,800
Purchases	48	45	460	1,000	1,000
Gross profit	47	55	540	1,400	1,800
Production overheads	8	9	85	220	260
Sales overheads	10	9	90	210	240
Administrative overheads	11	12	101	245	260
Net profit	18	25	264	725	1,040

2.3 Some explanations of the figures will demonstrate the difference between these management accounts and the published accounts we looked at earlier. The most important thing to remember is that management accounts are for *internal* use only. Published company accounts, by comparison, are for shareholders and other interested third parties and are required to meet specific content and disclosure requirements.

(a) *Month*. These are the actual figures for the month.

    (b) *Budget*. The budgeted figures for the month may have been seasonally adjusted or they may be just the total figure for the year, divided by twelve.

    (c) *Year to date*. These are the actual figures for the year up to the end of June.

    (d) *Budget for year*. This is, say, the budgeted figure for the year adjusted for the actual figures to date.

    (e) *Year plan*. This is the original budget for the year.

2.4   The breakdown of costs and expenses shown in management accounts is at the discretion of the management. The way the figures are presented will depend on what kind of information the managers require to control the business. The allocation of costs to the various profit and loss account categories in a published profit and loss account will be much more restricted and we will look at how both income and costs are recorded in the appropriate accounts in a later section of this chapter.

2.5   Management accounts may be broken down into separate departments, product lines or areas of management responsibility, depending on the structure of the business and the information required from the accounts.

2.6   We have now looked at the final accounts and some accounting principles, but before we look at how the information in the accounts is recorded and prepared, we should recap on the way an accounting system operates and in particular, how information is gathered, recorded and summarised.

3   THE ACCOUNTING SYSTEM

3.1   You should by now have a basic working knowledge of not only the accounting system, but also double-entry bookkeeping and ledger accounting. We can summarise the accounting system in a diagram (see next page) like the one shown in Chapter 1, but this time the fixed asset register, which we learnt about in Chapter 4, is added.

4   CLASSIFYING INCOME AND EXPENDITURE

4.1   We have seen in Paragraph 1.5 that in the profit and loss account, income and expenditure are classed under major headings, namely 'sales', 'cost of sales', 'distribution (and sales) expenses' and 'administrative expenses'. You should realise that these headings merely group income and costs together in a convenient manner because they are deemed to be of the same type in some way. The distinction between different types of item is more arbitrary than between capital and revenue items (which you should remember from Chapter 4), but it is still important that expense items are correctly recorded and classified, both for management control purposes and to give a clear picture of the affairs of the business to the outside world.

4.2   In general, it will be company or business policy which decides exactly how and where to record all items of income and expenditure. Accounts will be created within the accounting system which will be intended for specific items. The company will lay out guidelines which determine where types of income and expenditure should be posted and, once items have been coded for posting, a person in authority (such as an accounts supervisor) should mark the item as correctly coded. Where it is uncertain how an item should be coded, then the supervisor or a manager should be consulted. A manager or supervisor will also check posting summaries, or some other record, to ensure that no *misposting* (posting to the wrong account) has taken place.

SOURCE DOCUMENTS

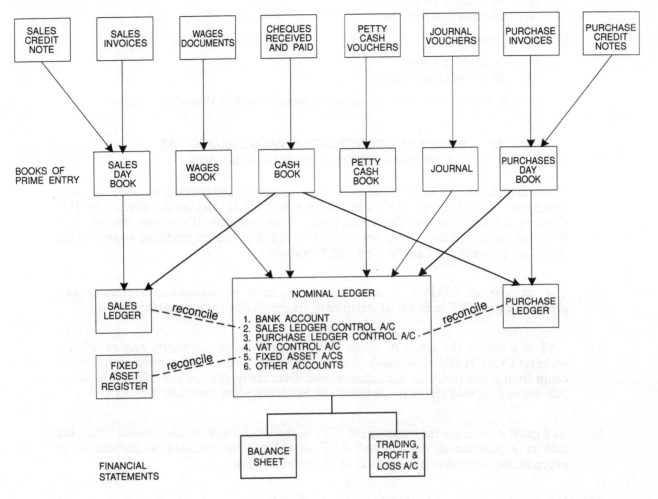

4.3 It may sometimes be necessary to split a single item into its different components for posting purposes. In any case, it is frequently the case that the prime document used for posting is stamped with a grid on which the account numbers are marked; alternatively a 'posting slip' may be stuck on the document, showing the same information.

4.4 You have already examined posting to some extent in your previous studies. You should now know how to post transactions to the ledger accounts, using double-entry bookkeeping. However, you were always told which account to post to; the Unit 5 Exercises and Assignments in the *Financial Accounting* Workbook will test your ability to decide where to post income and expense items. The list given below shows the other expenses which will appear under the profit and loss account headings shown earlier. As already mentioned, we will look at cost of sales in Chapter 7.

(a) *Selling and distribution expenses.* These are expenses associated with the process of selling and delivering goods to customers. They include the following items.

    (i)   Salaries of a sales director and sales management
    (ii)   Salaries and commissions of salesmen
    (iii) Travelling and entertainment expenses of salesmen
    (iv) Marketing costs (for example advertising and sales promotion expenses)
    (v)   Costs of running and maintaining delivery vans
    (vi) Discounts allowed to customers for early payment of their debts
    (vii) Bad debts written off (see Chapter 1)

(b) *Administration expenses.* These are the expenses of providing management and administration for the business. They include the following items.

    (i)   Salaries of directors, management and office staff
    (ii)   Rent and rates

(iii)   Insurance
(iv)   Telephone and postage
(v)   Printing and stationery
(vi)   Heating and lighting

(c) *Finance expenses*

(i)   Interest on a loan
(ii)   Bank overdraft interest

Note that in limited company accounts, interest *must* be shown separately.

5   SSAP 5 ACCOUNTING FOR VALUE ADDED TAX
Centrally assessed 6/94, 6/95, 12/95, 12/96, 6/97

5.1   If you completed the AAT Foundation stage, you will have covered some of the basic aspects of value added tax (VAT), including how VAT is calculated, collected by HM Customs & Excise and recorded in the books of the company. If you have not, you will find that the principles of VAT are covered in Unit 8 at the Intermediate stage (see the BPP *Cost Accounting II* Tutorial Text and Workbook).

5.2   The purpose of SSAP 5 is to achieve uniformity of accounting treatment and presentation of VAT in financial statements. Its provisions are summarised below.

5.3   VAT is a tax on the *supply* of goods and services. The tax authority responsible for collecting VAT is HM Customs & Excise. Tax is collected at each transfer point in the chain from prime producer to final consumer. Eventually, the consumer bears the tax in full and any tax paid earlier in the chain can be recovered by the trader who paid it.

5.4   As a general principle the treatment of VAT in the accounts of a trader should reflect his role as a collector of the tax and VAT should not be included in income or in expenditure, whether it is of a capital or of a revenue nature.

5.5   Where the trader *bears the VAT himself*, as in the following cases, this should be reflected in the accounts.

(a)   Persons *not registered* for VAT will suffer VAT on inputs (purchases). This will effectively increase the cost of their consumable materials and their fixed assets and this must be reflected in the books of the trader.

(b)   Registered persons who also carry on *exempted activities* will have a residue of VAT which falls directly on them. In this situation the costs to which this residue applies will be inflated by the irrecoverable VAT.

(c)   *Non-deductible inputs* will be borne by all traders (such as tax on cars bought and not for resale, and entertaining expenses).

5.6   SSAP 5 *Accounting for value added tax* states the following.

(a)   Turnover shown in the profit and loss account should *exclude* VAT on taxable outputs (sales). If gross turnover must be shown then the VAT in that figure must also be shown as a deduction in arriving at the turnover exclusive of VAT.

(b)   *Irrecoverable VAT* allocated to fixed assets and other items separately disclosed should be included in their cost where material and practical.

(c)   The net amount *due to (or from)* HM Customs & Excise should be included in the total for creditors (or debtors), and need not be separately disclosed.

6   SSAP 13 ACCOUNTING FOR RESEARCH AND DEVELOPMENT
Centrally assessed 6/96

6.1   In your Foundation stage studies, and in Unit 4: *Capital Transactions*, you have been concerned with the distinction between revenue items, which must be expensed in the profit and loss account, and capital items, which are capitalised in the balance sheet and depreciated through the profit and loss account. In this section, we examine a similar problem in relation to research and development (R & D) expenditure.

6.2   In many companies, especially those which produce food, or 'scientific' products such as medicines, or 'high technology' products, the expenditure on research and development is considerable. When R & D is a large item of cost, its accounting treatment may have a significant influence on the profits of a business and its balance sheet valuation.

6.3   SSAP 13 defines research and development expenditure as falling into one or more of the following categories.

(a)   *Pure research* is original research to obtain new scientific or technical knowledge or understanding. There is no clear commercial end in view and such research work does not have a practical application. Businesses might carry out this type of research in the hope that it will provide new knowledge which can subsequently be exploited.

(b)   *Applied research* is original research work which also seeks to obtain new scientific or technical knowledge, but which has a specific practical aim or application (for example research on improvements in the effectiveness of toothpastes or medicines). Applied research may develop from 'pioneering' pure research, but many companies have full-time research teams working on applied research projects.

(c)   *Development* is the use of existing scientific and technical knowledge to produce new (or substantially improved) products or systems, prior to starting commercial production operations.

6.4   The dividing line between each of these categories will often be indistinct in practice, and some expenditure might be classified as research or as development. It may be even more difficult to distinguish development costs from production costs. For example, if a prototype model of a new product is developed and then sold to a customer, the costs of the prototype will include both development and production expenditure.

6.5   SSAP 13 states that, although there may be practical difficulties in isolating research costs and development costs, there is a difference of principle in the method of accounting for each type of expenditure.

(a)   Expenditure on *pure and applied research* is usually a continuing operation which is necessary to ensure a company's survival. One accounting period does not gain more than any other from such work, and it is therefore appropriate that research costs should be written off as they are incurred (in the year of expenditure).

(b)   The *development* of new and improved products is different, because development expenditure is incurred with a particular commercial aim in view and in the reasonable expectation of earning profits or reducing costs. In these circumstances it is appropriate that development costs should be deferred (capitalised) and matched against the future revenues.

6.6   SSAP 13 attempts to restrict indiscriminate deferrals of development expenditure and states that development costs may only be deferred to future periods, when the following criteria are met.

(a)   There must be a *clearly defined development project*, and the related expenditure on this project must be separately identifiable.

(b)   The expected outcome of the project must have been assessed, and there should be reasonable certainty that:

(i)   it is *technically feasible*; and

(ii)   it is *commercially viable*, having regard to market conditions, competition, public opinion and consumer and environmental legislation.

(c) The eventual *profits* from the developed product or system should reasonably be expected to cover the past and future development costs.

(d) The company should have *adequate resources* to complete the development project.

If any of these conditions are not satisfied, the development costs should be written off in the year of expenditure.

6.7 Where development expenditure is deferred to future periods, its *amortisation* (ie depreciation) should begin with the commencement of production, and should then be written off over the period in which the product is expected to be sold.

6.8 Deferred development expenditure should be reviewed at the end of every accounting period. If the conditions which justified the deferral of the expenditure no longer apply or are considered doubtful, the deferred expenditure should be written off, to the extent that it is now considered to be irrecoverable. Development expenditure once written off can also be *reinstated*, if the uncertainties which had led to its being written off no longer apply.

6.9 You may wonder whether *market research* can be included in development costs. In fact, market research is excluded from R & D by SSAP 13. However a company can *defer* market research costs under the accruals concept (if it is prudent so to do) but it must be disclosed entirely separately from deferred development expenditure.

6.10 The provisions of SSAP 13 in Paragraph 6.6 do *not* extend to the following cases.

(a) Expenditure on *tangible fixed assets* acquired or constructed to provide facilities for research and/or development activities should be capitalised and depreciated over their useful lives in the usual way. However, the *depreciation* may be capitalised as part of deferred development expenditure if the development work for which the assets are used meets the criteria given above.

(b) Expenditure incurred in locating *mineral deposits* in extractive industries is outside the scope of SSAP 13.

(c) Expenditure incurred where there is a *firm contract*:

(i) to carry out development work on behalf of third parties on such terms that the related expenditure is to be fully reimbursed; or

(ii) to develop and manufacture at an agreed price which has been calculated to reimburse expenditure on development as well as on manufacture,

is not to be treated as deferred development expenditure. Any such expenditure which has not been reimbursed at the balance sheet date should be included in work in progress.

Example: Research and development

6.11 Milburn plc, a large drug company, has incurred the following expenditure during the year to 31 March 19X1.

(a) £500,000 was spent on advertising a new brand of paracetamol which has just come on to the market.

(b) The company has spent £2.5 million during the year to develop a new arthritis drug. Expenditure in 19X2 is expected to be £1.5 million. The drug will go on sale in 19X3 and it is expected to be a market leader for four years. Total income is expected to exceed costs. The project is a technical success; trials have been carried out and a worldwide licence obtained. The company has large cash reserves with which to complete the project.

Task

Show the entries necessary to record the above transactions in the profit and loss account and balance sheet of Milburn Ltd.

Solution: Research and development

6.12 Under SSAP 13 the expenditure should be treated in the following ways.

(a) The expenditure on advertising does not qualify as development expenditure and it should be written off in the profit and loss account in 19X1.

(b) The money spent on developing a new arthritis drug qualifies as development expenditure under all the criteria. The balance sheet and profit and loss account entries for the next few years will be as follows.

BALANCE SHEET

	19X1 £'000	19X2 £'000	19X3 £'000	19X4 £'000	19X5 £'000	19X6 £'000
Deferred development expenditure	2,500	4,000	4,000	4,000	4,000	4,000
Amortisation	-	-	1,000	2,000	3,000	4,000
	2,500	4,000	3,000	2,000	1,000	-

PROFIT AND LOSS ACCOUNT

Amortisation of development expenditure	-	-	1,000	1,000	1,000	1,000

7 SSAP 21 ACCOUNTING FOR LEASES AND HIRE PURCHASE CONTRACTS
Centrally assessed 12/96

7.1 Where goods are acquired other than on immediate cash terms, arrangements have to be made in respect of the future payments on those goods. In the simplest case of credit sales, the purchaser is allowed a period of time (say one month) to settle the outstanding amount and the normal accounting procedure in respect of debtors/creditors will be adopted. However, in recent years there has been considerable growth in hire purchase and leasing agreements. SSAP 21 *Accounting for leases and hire purchase contracts* standardises the accounting treatment and disclosure of assets held under lease or hire purchase.

Type of lease and HP agreement

7.2 In a leasing transaction there is a *contract* between the lessor and the lessee for the hire of an asset. The lessor retains legal ownership but conveys to the lessee the right to use the asset for an agreed period of time in return for specified rentals. SSAP 21 recognises two types of lease.

(a) A *finance lease* transfers substantially all the risks and rewards of ownership to the lessee. Although strictly the leased asset remains the property of the lessor, in substance the lessee may be considered to have acquired the asset and to have financed the acquisition by obtaining a loan from the lessor.

(b) An *operating lease* is any lease which is not a finance lease. An operating lease has the character of a rental agreement with the lessor usually being responsible for repairs and maintenance of the asset. Often these are relatively short-term agreements with the same asset being leased, in succession, to different lessees.

7.3 A *finance lease* is very similar in substance to a *hire purchase agreement*. (The difference in law is that under a hire purchase agreement the customer eventually, after paying an agreed number of instalments, becomes entitled to exercise an option to purchase the asset. Under a leasing agreement, ownership remains forever with the lessor.) In this chapter the user of an asset will often be referred to simply as the lessee, and the supplier as the lessor. You should bear in mind that identical requirements apply in the case of hirers and vendors respectively under hire purchase agreements.

Accounting for leases: lessees and lessors

7.4 *Operating leases* do not really pose an accounting problem. The lessee pays amounts periodically to the lessor and these are charged to the profit and loss account. The lessor treats the leased asset as a fixed asset and depreciates it in the normal way. Rentals received from the lessee are credited to the profit and loss account in the lessor's books.

7.5 For assets held under *finance leases or hire purchase* this accounting treatment would not disclose the reality of the situation. If a lessor leases out an asset on a finance lease, the asset will probably never be seen on his premises or used in his business again. It would be inappropriate for a lessor to record such an asset as a fixed asset. In reality, what he owns is a stream of cash flows receivable from the lessee. The asset is a *debtor* rather than a fixed asset.

7.6 Similarly, a lessee may use a finance lease to fund the 'acquisition' of a major asset which he will then use in his business perhaps for many years. The substance of the transaction is that he has acquired a fixed asset, and this is reflected in the accounting treatment prescribed by SSAP 21, even though in law the lessee never becomes the owner of the asset.

7.7 In light of the above, SSAP 21 requires that, when an asset changes hands under a finance lease or HP agreement, lessor and lessee should account for the transaction as though it were a credit sale. In the lessee's books therefore:

DEBIT   Asset account
CREDIT Lessor (liability) account

7.8 The amount to be recorded in this way is the capital cost or fair value of the asset. This may be taken as the amount which the lessee might expect to pay for the asset in a cash transaction.

7.9 The asset should be *depreciated* over the shorter of:

(a) the lease term; and
(b) its useful life.

Apportionment of rental payments

7.10 When the lessee makes a rental payment it will comprise two elements.

(a) An *interest charge* on the finance provided by the lessor. This proportion of each payment is interest payable and interest receivable in the profit and loss accounts of the lessee and lessor respectively.

(b) A repayment of part of the *capital cost* of the asset. In the lessee's books this proportion of each rental payment must be debited to the lessor's account to reduce the outstanding liability. In the lessor's books, it must be credited to the lessee's account to reduce the amount owing (the debit of course is to cash).

7.11 The accounting problem is to decide what proportion of each instalment paid by the lessee represents interest, and what proportion represents a repayment of the capital advanced by the lessor. There are various methods of determining this question which is beyond the scope of this text.

Accounting for leases

7.12 What is the difference, in accounting terms, between

(a) buying an asset outright;
(b) renting an asset under an operating lease; and
(c) obtaining an asset under a finance lease?

7.13 Suppose an asset can be obtained by any of these methods and the following terms apply.

Cash price = £7,710
Finance lease price = £10,000 (finance charge is therefore £10,000 – £7,710 = £2,290)
Finance lease terms = £2,000 deposit plus remainder in four equal instalments
Operating lease terms = rent of £1,500 pa

7.14 The accounting entries for the lessee would be as follows. (Depreciation is ignored here, but the asset should be depreciated over a *maximum* of four years.)

(a) *Cash purchase*

DEBIT	Fixed asset account	£7,710	
CREDIT	Bank		£7,710

Being cash purchase of a fixed asset

(b) *Finance lease*

DEBIT	Fixed asset account	£7,710	
CREDIT	Finance lease creditor		£7,710

Being record of purchase price of asset

DEBIT	Finance lease creditor	£2,000	
CREDIT	Bank		£2,000

Being payment of deposit

DEBIT	Interest payable	£572.50	★
	Finance lease creditor	£1,427.50	
CREDIT	Bank		£2,000

Being payment of instalment (repeated every year for four years)

★ Calculated as £2,290 ÷ 4 years, but here are other methods of allocating finance charges, beyond the scope of this unit.

(c) *Operating lease*

DEBIT	Rental payable	£1,500	
CREDIT	Bank		£1,500

Being rental payment under operating lease

7.15 You can see that (ignoring depreciation), the only effect in (a) is on the balance sheet, whereas in (c) the only impact is on the profit and loss account. Under the finance lease, however, the balance sheet will show both the cost of the asset (and depreciation) *and* the finance lease creditor balance, which at the end of the first year will be £7,710 – £2,000 – £1,427.50 = £4,282.50. Only the capital part of the lease payments are shown as a creditor balance because, in theory, the lessee could pay off the rest of the capital balance at the beginning of the next year and so no more finance charges would be payable. The profit and loss account will show the interest (finance) charge of £572.50.

7.16 For the lessor, the entries would be reversed (ie show a finance lease debtor and finance charge income) but no fixed asset is recorded.

Key points in this chapter

- Published *financial accounts* comprise a balance sheet and a profit and loss account.

- *Management accounts* are produced to help the managers guide and control the business.

- Income and expenditure must be *posted* to the correct accounts, otherwise the accounts will be meaningless and the managers will not be able to control the business.

- SSAP 5 *Accounting for value added tax* gives rules for the treatment of VAT in accounts, the most important of which is that all items in the accounts should be shown net of recoverable VAT.

- SSAP 13 *Accounting for research and development* distinguishes between research costs and development costs, of which the latter may be capitalised and matched against future revenues.

- SSAP 21 *Accounting for leases and hire purchase contracts* divides leases into two categories: finance leases and operating leases. You only need to know in general terms about the differences between these types of lease. You will not be expected to account for a lease.

For practice on the points covered in this chapter you should now attempt the Practice Exercises in Session 5 of the Financial Accounting Workbook

6 Accruals and prepayments

This chapter covers the following topics.

1   Introduction

2   Accruals

3   Prepayments

4   Obtaining information

1   INTRODUCTION

1.1   When income and expenditure is recorded, it is usually because an invoice has been received or an invoice has been issued, and the expense or income must therefore be recognised. The same applies when purchases or sales are made for cash. At the end of the accounting period, however, it may be that some bills have not been received, although it is known that the expense has been incurred. The liability will therefore not be recorded until the following period. Similarly, an invoice may have been received and paid during the year, but it may cover part of the following year. In both these cases, there is a problem as the amounts do not relate wholly to the *period* in which they were recorded.

1.2   As we saw earlier, the *accruals concept* states that income and expenditure should be matched to each other and recognised as they are earned or incurred, not when money is received or paid. *Accruals*, or accrued expenses, are expenses which are charged against the profits of a particular period, even though they have not yet been paid off, because they were incurred in that period. *Prepayments* are payments which have been made in one accounting period, but should not be wholly or partly charged against profit until a later period, because they relate to that later period.

1.3   Before we go on to look at how accruals and prepayments are identified and calculated in detail, here are two very simple examples to demonstrate the principles of accruals and prepayments.

Example: Accrual

1.4   Cleverley plc started in business as a paper plate and cup manufacturer on 1 January 19X2, making up accounts to 31 December 19X2. The electricity bills received were as follows.

	£
30 April 19X2	5,279.47
31 July 19X2	4,663.80
31 October 19X2	4,117.28
31 January 19X3	6,491.52

What should the electricity charge be for the year ended 31 December 19X2?

Solution: Accrual

1.5   The total of the three invoices received during 19X2 was £14,060.55, but this is not the full charge for the year: the November and December electricity charge was not invoiced until the end of January. To show the correct charge for the year, it is necessary to accrue the charge for November and December based on the bill received in January. The charge for 19X2 will be:

	£
Paid in year	14,060.55
Accrual ($^2/_3$ × £6,491.52)	4,327.68
	18,388.23

1.6   The double entry for the accrual will be:

DEBIT	Electricity account (P & L a/c)	£4,327.68	
CREDIT	Accruals (balance sheet)		£4,327.68

Example: Prepayment

1.7   Hillyard Ltd opened for business on 1 January 19X4 in a new shop which was on a 20 year lease. The rent is payable quarterly in advance and amounts to £20,000 per year. The payments were made on what are know as the 'quarter-days' (except for the first payment) as follows.

	£
1 January 19X4	5,000.00
25 March 19X4	5,000.00
24 June 19X4	5,000.00
29 September 19X4	5,000.00
25 December 19X4	5,000.00

What will the rental charge be for the year ended 31 December 19X4?

Solution: Prepayment

1.8 The total amount paid in the year is £25,000. The yearly rental, however, is only £20,000. The last payment was almost entirely a prepayment (give or take a few days) as it is payment in advance for the first three months of 19X5. The charge for 19X4 is therefore:

	£
Paid in year	25,000.00
Prepayment	(5,000.00)
	20,000.00

1.9 The double entry for this prepayment is:

DEBIT	Prepayment (balance sheet)	£5,000.00	
CREDIT	Rent account (P & L a/c)		£5,000.00

1.10 You can see from the double entry shown for both these examples that the other side of the entry is taken to the balance sheet. *Prepayments* are included in *debtors* in current assets in the balance sheet. Prepayments are assets in the sense that they represent the money that has been paid out in advance of the expense being incurred. Similarly, *accruals* are included in *creditors* in current liabilities as they represent liabilities which have been incurred but not yet invoiced.

1.11 In each of the above examples, as with all prepayments and accruals, the double entry will be *reversed* in the following period. It may help to see the accounts in question.

ELECTRICITY ACCOUNT

19X2		£	*19X2*		£
30.4	Cash	5,279.47	31.12	P & L account	18,388.23
31.7	Cash	4,663.80			
31.10	Cash	4,117.28			
31.12	Balance c/d (accrual)	4,327.68			
		18,388.23			18,388.23
19X3			*19X3*		
			1.1	Balance b/d	4,327.68

RENT ACCOUNT

19X2		£	*19X2*		£
1.1	Cash	5,000.00	31.12	P & L account	20,000.00
25.3	Cash	5,000.00	31.12	Balance c/d	
24.6	Cash	5,000.00		(prepayment)	5,000.00
29.9	Cash	5,000.00			
25.12	Cash	5,000.00			
		25,000.00			25,000.00
19X3			*19X3*		
1.1	Balance b/d	5,000.00			

1.12 In the next two sections of this chapter we will look at some of the practical aspects of identifying and calculating accruals. The basic principles as described above will apply at all times.

2   ACCRUALS
Centrally assessed 6/94 - 6/97

2.1   In this section we will go through some of the *practical procedures* you might be required to carry out to identify and record accruals. First of all, here is a list of procedures.

(a)   Review the accruals listing for the previous year and consider whether similar conditions exist for each of the relevant accounts. This list may be used as the basis of the current year's accruals listing.

(b)   Review every account which relates to income and expenditure. Examine the transactions passing through the accounts and identify any accounts where fewer invoices have been received than expected (eg only three quarterly telephone bills).

(c)   Review all invoices received after the year end to identify any amounts which relate to the year in question (eg an electricity bill received one month after the year end which covers a whole quarter).

(d)   Collect together and compare all the information found and calculate the relevant accruals. Compare the final list with the previous year's accruals again to check for any omissions.

Accruals listing from previous year

2.2   Many businesses run on a very *regular basis* from year to year. It is frequently the case that the same transactions recur year after year, often at the same time each year. For the accounting technician seeking to identify all accruals, this regularity gives an ideal starting point in that the accruals calculated for the previous year will give a strong indication of those required for the current year.

2.3   As an example of a complete listing, consider that given below.

Accruals Listing Year ended 31 December 19X6		£
A/C No.	Name	
P001	Purchases	32,148.42
E002	Electricity	927.28
T004	Telephone	1,427.19
G011	Gas	2,119.40
I001	Bank interest	1,307.07
S007	Salaries	10,172.29
W001	Wages	9,428.56
E012	Mileage allowance	322.27
E013	Salesmen's expenses	584.71
C100	TOTAL	58,437.19

Note. The figure for purchases represents goods received into stock where no invoice has yet been received. We will look at stock accruals in more detail in the next chapter.

2.4 The types of expenditure shown in this listing are usually very regular in nature and therefore accruals would be expected to arise again in the following year.

Review expense accounts

2.5 A review of the expense accounts will often reveal the need for an accrual where an invoice relating to the current year is not received until after the year end. This is often the case with some utilities (electricity, gas) as payments are usually made quarterly and the end of a quarter may not coincide with the year end of the business. For example, you might examine the electricity account for the year ended 31 December 19X7.

ACCOUNT NAME	E0002 ELECTRICITY		DATE 0202X8
		Amount £	*Balance* £
0101X7	Balance	(927.28)	(927.28)
2802X7	Invoice	2,781.84	1,854.56
3005X7	Invoice	2,417.38	4,271.94
3008X7	Invoice	2,559.61	6,831.55
3011X7	Invoice	3,172.31	10,003.86

2.6 You can see that, although four quarterly invoices have been received during the year, the last one does not include the December charge for electricity and therefore an accrual is necessary. Note that it is not sufficient to simply carry forward the same accrual year after year as consumption may change, as it has here, with the charge for electricity increasing towards the year end.

Review past year end invoices

2.7 It may be the case that a review of the accounts and an examination of the accruals listing for the previous year will fail to highlight some expenses which should be accrued, perhaps because they are unusual or unexpected. To avoid missing such expenses, all invoices received after the year end should be checked, to ensure that they do not relate to the previous period. This exercise should be continued for a reasonable amount of time after the year end, although within the bounds of practicality, eg up until the date the accounts are finalised.

2.8 Supposing that you carried out this exercise while preparing accounts for the year ended 31 December 19X7 and found the two invoices shown here (among others).

WORKBASE OFFICE SUPPLIES LTD

63 Conduit street
Liverpool
L1 6NN

Telephone: 0151-432 2222
Fax: 0151-432 2210

VAT Reg No. 924 4614 29

Invoice No.	7012
Order No.	1137
Account No.	R001
Date/Tax point	31 January 19X8

Rabbit Fast Food Franchises Ltd
62 Hellon Avenue
Bournley
L24 6BS

Product code	Description	Quantity	Unit price £ p	Total amount £ p
P11110	Photocopier rental 1.11.X7 - 31.1.X8	N/A	450.00	450.00

Comments:		NET TOTAL	450.00
Your photocopier is due for a service on 31 May 19X8		VAT @ 17.5%	78.75
		TOTAL	528.75

Registered office: 63 Conduit Street, Liverpool L1 6NN   Registered No: 822 4742

ERGONOME LTD   **SALES INVOICE**

Fonda House, 12 Angriman Street
Pleading, Lincs

TO: Rabbit Fast Food
      Franchises Ltd
      62 Hellon Avenue
      Bownley
      L24 6BS

F.A.O   Purchase Ledger

Invoice No:	8742
Account No.	DEF 2
Date/Tax pt:	28.02.X8

	Price £ p
Answering service 1 daytime 1.12.19X7 - 28.2.19X8	2,000.00
Night answering service 1.12.19X7 - 28.2.19X8	500.00
	2,500.00
VAT at 17.5%	437.50
	2,937.50

VAT Reg: 3 495 0721

2.9 Both the photocopier and the answering service were used for the first time this year and therefore no accrual would have been anticipated based on the previous year's figures. As you can see, however, these invoices relate in part to the year ended 31 December 19X7.

Calculating accruals

2.10 Once the need for an accrual has been identified, you must calculate the correct amount of the accrual. Two different circumstances may arise here, generally relating to the *timing* of the accruals calculation.

(a) It may be that an invoice has been received after the year end but before the preparation of the accounts, which gives an actual charge for a given period. In this case, the only calculation made will be that required to *apportion* the charge to the period in question. For example, from the invoice given above from Workbase Office Supplies Ltd, it can be seen that the amount of the charge relating to 19X7 is:

$$\frac{2\ months}{3\ months} \times £450.00 = £300.00$$

$$(or\ \frac{61\ days}{92\ days} \times £450.00 = £298.37)$$

(b) Alternatively, an invoice may not be received by the time the accounts are prepared. In such cases, it is necessary to *estimate* the accrual based on current or expected consumption. For example, when we looked at the electricity account in Paragraph 2.5 above, we might have decided that consumption in December has been the same as in the previous three months. We would therefore calculate the accrual as:

$$\frac{1\ month}{3\ months} \times £3,172.31 = £1,057.44$$

Note. Be careful not to include VAT in the calculation; this is posted to a separate account.

2.11 Whatever method is used to estimate or calculate the accrual, it should be a reasonable approximation to the actual charge and the method should be applied *consistently* from year to year.

3 PREPAYMENTS
Centrally assessed 6/94 - 6/97

3.1 Many of the principles we discussed in relation to identifying and calculating accruals apply to identifying and calculating prepayments as well. The major practical difference, of course, is that invoices have been received and paid during the year in the case of prepayments. As the information is already within the accounting system at the year end, no post year end review of invoices is necessary, but the following procedures should be carried out.

(a) Review the list of prepayments from the previous year end. Once again, regular payments such as those for rent, uniform business rate or water rates, which are normally paid in advance, should show up.

(b) Review all expense accounts during the year to identify any prepaid expenses. During the year, it is often helpful to make a note when any invoice is paid which partly relates to the next accounting period. This procedure could easily be incorporated into the preparation of monthly management accounts.

(c) Calculate and list all the prepayments. Compare the list with that of the previous year and check that there are no omissions.

Prepayments listing from previous year

3.2 The listings below gives an idea of the type of expenses which might be prepaid.

Prepayments Listing Year ended 31 December 19X7		£
A/C No.	Name	
U004	Unified business rate	11,407.18
W001	Water rates	1,773.21
R003	Rent	6,400.00
T004	Telephone	101.72
I001	Insurance - building	3,211.96
I002	Insurance - general	1,195.20
P010	Plant hire	429.50
D100	TOTAL	24,518.77

3.3 The listing will give you a starting point from which to work.

Review expense accounts

3.4 As in the case with accruals, all the expense accounts should be reviewed, to check whether any contain prepaid expenses. The types of regular payments shown above are often paid in advance, but so are most one-off expenses, which may be harder to spot.

Calculation of prepayments

3.5 Prepayments are usually very straightforward to calculate, because the expenses can be apportioned on a time basis. In the case of the uniform business rate, for example, suppose that £22,472.58 was paid by a business on 1 April 19X8 for the year to 31 March 19X9. The business, which is preparing accounts to 31 December 19X8, has prepaid for the three months in 19X9 and therefore the prepayment is calculated as:

$^3/_{12} \times £22,472.58 = £5,618.15$

As a further example (for the same business) suppose an insurance bill for £9,473.80 was paid on 1 August 19X8 for the year ended 31 July 19X9. Seven months worth of the bill relates to 19X9, and so the prepayment is:

$^7/_{12} \times £9,473.80 = £5,526.38$

3.6 You may have noticed that, in both the accruals and prepayments listing there is an amount under the heading of telephone. You can see why a prepayment *and* an accrual might arise by looking at the telephone bill below.

```
          NATIONAL                    Telephone Account
          TELECOM
                                    National Telecommunications plc VAT No. 234 5678 12
                                            Customer account number

      BELL HOUSE                                    QQ 1234 5678 PPP1 A1
      RINGROAD                                              30/11/X7
   — — LONDON                                              (TAX POINT)
      WE7 7TT

      BILL ENQUIRIES 0171-000 2222
                                              Brierly plc
      NOTIFICATION OF PAYMENT                 Unit 4A
      (24 HOURS) 0444 098765                  Riverside Park
      — — — — — — — — — — — —                 London NW1

      SALES/GENERAL
      ENQUIRIES    0171-000 3333
```

CHARGES FOR TELEPHONE SERVICE ON 0171-000 3333

		£	£
CURRENT CHARGES			
Rental-System	01/12/X7 to 28/02/X8		56.84
Dialled Calls			
Meter Reading	28/11/X7	17,228	
Meter Reading	27/08/X7	10,978	
Number of units @ 4.20p		6,250	262.50
Low User Rental Rebate			
Total of Current Charges (Excl VAT)			319.34
Value Added Tax at 17.50%			55.88
Total of Current Charges (Incl VAT)			375.22

£ 375.22

Total Amount Due

PLEASE SEE OVERLEAF FOR PAYMENT AND CUSTOMER SERVICE INFORMATION

```
 G Girobank              PAYMENT SLIP          Bank Giro Credit

 135   Customer account number   Credit account number   Amount      By transfer from Girobank a/c no.
 205     12345678 PPP1            1473228         £ 375.22

 Cashiers Stamp                                                    CASH
 and initials
              Signature _____   Date _____             CHEQ

                 43-80-63      MIDWEST BANK plc                £
                               Head Office Collection Account

                                                                  NATIONAL
  Items    Fee    Please do not write or mark below this line or fold this payment slip   TELECOM

 Cece 12345678 PPP1  1473228
```

3.7 Assuming that no further bill has been received, at 31 December 19X7 the following calculations will be made.

Prepayment: rental for January and February 19X8 = $^2/_3 \times £56.84 = £37.89$

Accrual: call charges for December 19X7 = $^1/_3 \times £262.50 = £87.50$

Payments received in advance

3.8 This is a convenient point to mention the treatment of payments received by a business in advance. This arises often with *clubs* which receive subscriptions in advance.

3.9 A payment received in advance is the opposite of a prepayment. It is, in effect, *deferred income*. It is treated as a *liability* in the accounts of the current period and as *income* in the accounting period to which it relates.

4   OBTAINING INFORMATION

4.1   So far in this chapter we have assumed that you, as an Accounting Technician, will be performing the task of identifying and calculating prepayments and accruals. In larger organisations, it is not unusual to find that the managers of individual divisions or companies will be asked to supply such information at the period end. The information is then collated in the central accounts department.

4.2   Where such delegation takes place, it is important that the managers know exactly what information is needed and what, if any, supporting documentation is required. Good communications need to be maintained between the division managers and the central accounting staff. (This should of course apply at all times, not just at the year end when such accounting information is required.)

4.3   One way to ensure that correct and complete accruals and prepayments information is sent by the managers is to send them a checklist or listing sheet which lays out all the information they should consider. An example of such a checklist is given below. It would be usual to request copies of all supporting documentation for the divisional accruals and prepayments as an aid to the central accounting function, and also to provide information for the company auditors. (The auditors will want to check all the figures in the accounts, including the accruals and prepayments.)

ACCRUALS/PREPAYMENTS CHECKLIST

1. Stock accruals: all purchases made pre-year end, goods received but no invoice. ☐

   ENCLOSE COPY GRNS

2. All relevant expense accounts

   (a) last bills before the year end; and/or ☐

   (b) bills just after the year end; and ☐

   (c) list any others ☐

   ENCLOSE COPY INVOICES

3. All expense prepayments: last bills before year end ☐

   ENCLOSE COPY INVOICES

4. Full listing. Cross reference to supporting documents and any calculations or explanations.

4.4   There are other important matters to bear in mind.

   (a)   Managers should be warned well in advance in writing about the information they are required to supply.

   (b)   Details of how to complete the exercise should be supplied to them in writing and they should be encouraged to contact the central accounts department with any queries.

   (c)   All communications should be polite and tactful.

Key points in this chapter

- An *accrual* is a liability at the year end (a creditor in the balance sheet). It is an expense which has not yet been entered in an expense account because no invoice has yet been recorded at the year end.

- A *prepayment* is similar to a debtor and is shown as a current asset in the balance sheet. It is an expense which has already been entered in an expense account (because an invoice has been received) but which is not a part of expenditure relating to the current year.

- The *practical difficulties* involved in identifying and calculating accruals and prepayments include:

  o ensuring completeness;
  o checking and collating information from divisions.

For practice on the points covered in this chapter you should now attempt the Practice Exercises in Session 6 of the Financial Accounting Workbook

Part D
Preparing accounts

7 The trial balance and stocks

This chapter covers the following topics.

1 The trial balance

2 Suspense accounts

3 Cost of goods sold

4 Accounting for opening and closing stocks

5 Stocktaking and stock accruals

6 Valuing stocks

---

1   THE TRIAL BALANCE

Centrally assessed 6/94 - 6/97

1.1   In Chapter 8 we will look at the problems faced when preparing accounts from incomplete records. First of all, we need to examine some of the basic procedures involved in balancing the ledger accounts off and preparing a trial balance. In very straightforward circumstances, where no complications arise, and where the records are complete, it is possible to prepare accounts directly from a trial balance. We referred to this situation in Section 9 of Chapter 1 and we go in to detail here. In Chapter 10 we will see that, in more complicated situations, it is necessary to *extend* the trial balance. In the rest of this chapter we will look at some of the complications involved with stocks.

The first step

1.2   Before you draw up a trial balance, you must have a collection of ledger accounts. We will use the accounts of R Kala, a sole trader. (Exactly the same principles will apply to limited companies.)

CASH

	£		£
Capital: R Kala	7,000	Rent	3,500
Bank loan	1,000	Shop fittings	2,000
Sales	10,000	Trade creditors	5,000
Debtors	2,500	Bank loan interest	100
		Incidental expenses	1,900
		Drawings	1,500
			14,000
		Balancing figure: the amount of cash left over after payments have been made	6,500
	20,500		20,500

CAPITAL (R KALA)

	£		£
		Cash	7,000

BANK LOAN

	£		£
		Cash	1,000

PURCHASES

	£		£
Trade creditors	5,000		

TRADE CREDITORS

	£		£
Cash	5,000	Purchases	5,000

RENT

	£		£
Cash	3,500		

SHOP FITTINGS

	£		£
Cash	2,000		

SALES

	£		£
		Cash	10,000
		Debtors	2,500

DEBTORS

	£		£
Sales	2,500	Cash	2,500

BANK LOAN INTEREST

	£		£
Cash	100		

INCIDENTAL EXPENSES

	£		£
Cash	1,900		

DRAWINGS ACCOUNT

	£		£
Cash	1,500		

1.3   The next step is to 'balance' each account.

Balancing ledger accounts

1.4   At the end of an accounting period, a balance is struck on each account in turn. This means that all the debits on the account are totalled and so are all the credits. If the total debits are greater than the total credits there is said to be a *debit balance* on the account; if the total credits are greater than the total debits then the account has a *credit balance*.

1.5   In our simple example, there is very little balancing to do.

(a)   Both the trade creditors account and the debtors account balance off to zero.
(b)   The cash account has a debit balance of £6,500.
(c)   The total on the sales account is £12,500, which is a credit balance.

Otherwise, the accounts have only one entry each, so there is no totalling to do to arrive at the balance on each account.

Collecting the balances

1.6   If the basic principle of double entry has been correctly applied throughout the period it will be found that the credit balances equal the debit balances in total. This can be illustrated by collecting together the balances on R Kala's accounts.

	Debit £	Credit £
Cash	6,500	
Capital		7,000
Bank loan		1,000
Purchases	5,000	
Trade creditors	-	-
Rent	3,500	
Shop fittings	2,000	
Sales		12,500
Debtors	-	-
Bank loan interest	100	
Other expenses	1,900	
Drawings	1,500	
	20,500	20,500

1.7   This list of balances is called the *trial balance*. It does not matter in what order the various accounts are listed, because the trial balance is not a document that a company *has* to prepare. It is just a method used to test the accuracy of the double entry bookkeeping methods.

What if the trial balance shows unequal debit and credit balances?

1.8 If the two columns of the trial balance are not equal, there must be an error in recording the transactions in the accounts. A trial balance, however, will *not* disclose the following types of errors.

(a) The complete *omission* of a transaction, because neither a debit nor a credit is made

(b) The posting of a debit or credit to the correct side of the ledger, but to a *wrong account*

(c) *Compensating errors* (eg an error of £100 is exactly cancelled by another £100 error elsewhere)

(d) *Errors of principle*, eg cash received from debtors being debited to the debtors account and credited to cash instead of the other way round

We will look at how to cope with problems which do show up on the trial balance in the next section.

Example: Trial balance

1.9 As at 30 March 19X7, your business has the following balances on its ledger accounts.

Accounts	Balance £
Bank loan	12,000 Cr
Cash	11,700 Dr
Capital	13,000 Cr
Rates	1,880 Dr
Trade creditors	11,200 Cr
Purchases	12,400 Dr
Sales	14,600 Cr
Sundry creditors	1,620 Cr
Debtors	12,000 Dr
Bank loan interest	1,400 Dr
Other expenses	11,020 Dr
Vehicles	2,020 Dr

During 31 March 19X7 the business made the following transactions.

(a) Bought materials for £1,000, £500 for cash and £500 for credit
(b) Made £1,040 sales, £800 of which was for credit
(c) Paid wages to shop assistants of £260 in cash

Task

Draw up a trial balance showing the balances as at the end of 31 March 19X7.

Solution: Trial balance

1.10 First it is necessary to put the original balances into a trial balance, identifying which are debit and which are credit balances. At the same time we can check that the total debit and credit balances are equal.

Account	Debit £	Credit £
Bank loan		12,000
Cash	11,700	
Capital		13,000
Rates	1,880	
Trade creditors		11,200
Purchases	12,400	
Sales		14,600
Sundry creditors		1,620
Debtors	12,000	
Bank loan interest	1,400	
Other expenses	11,020	
Vehicles	2,020	
	52,420	52,420

1.11 Now we must take account of the effects of the three transactions which took place on 31 March 19X7.

			£	£
(a)				
	DEBIT	Purchases	1,000	
	CREDIT	Cash		500
		Trade creditors		500
(b)				
	CREDIT	Sales		1,040
	DEBIT	Cash	240	
		Debtors	800	
(c)	DEBIT	Other expenses	260	
	CREDIT	Cash		260

1.12 When these figures are included in the trial balance, it becomes:

Account	Debit £	Credit £
Bank loan		12,000
Cash	11,180	
Capital		13,000
Rates	1,880	
Trade creditors		11,700
Purchases	13,400	
Sales		15,640
Sundry creditors		1,620
Debtors	12,800	
Bank loan interest	1,400	
Other expenses	11,280	
Vehicles	2,020	
	53,960	53,960

The trading, profit and loss account
Centrally assessed 6/94

1.13 The next step in the process of preparing the financial statements is to open up another ledger account, called the *trading, profit and loss account*. In it a business summarises its results for the period by gathering together all the ledger account balances relating to income and expenses. This account is still part of the double entry system, so the basic rule of double entry still applies: every debit must have an equal and opposite credit entry.

1.14 The trading, profit and loss account we open up is not the financial statement we are aiming for, even though it has the same name. The difference between the two is not very great, because they effectively contain similar information. However, the financial statement lays it out differently and may be much less detailed.

1.15 So what do we do with this new ledger account? The first step is to look through the ledger accounts and identify which ones relate to income and expenses. In the case of the earlier example R Kala, the income and expense accounts consist of purchases, rent, sales, bank loan interest, and other expenses.

1.16 The balances on these accounts are transferred to the new trading, profit and loss account. For example, the balance on the purchases account is £5,000 DR. To balance this to zero, we write in £5,000 CR. But to comply with the rule of double entry, there has to be a debit entry somewhere, so we write £5,000 DR in the trading, profit and loss account. Now the balance on the purchases account has been moved to the trading, profit and loss account.

1.17 If we do the same thing with all the income and expense accounts of R Kala (see the list of balances at Paragraph 1.6 above), the result is as follows.

PURCHASES

	£		£
Trade creditors	5,000	Trading, P & L a/c	5,000

RENT

	£		£
Cash	3,500	Trading, P & L a/c	3,500

SALES

	£		£
Trading, P & L a/c	12,500	Cash	10,000
		Debtors	2,500
	12,500		12,500

BANK LOAN INTEREST

	£		£
Cash	100	Trading, P & L a/c	100

OTHER EXPENSES

	£		£
Cash	1,900	Trading, P & L a/c	1,900

TRADING, PROFIT AND LOSS ACCOUNT

	£		£
Purchases	5,000	Sales	12,500
Rent	3,500		
Bank loan interest	100		
Other expenses	1,900		

(Note that the trading, profit and loss account has not yet been balanced off, but we will return to that later.)

1.18 If you look at the items we have gathered together in the trading, profit and loss account, they should strike a chord in your memory. They are the same items that we need to draw up the trading, profit and loss account in the form of a financial statement. With a little rearrangement they could be presented as follows.

R KALA
TRADING, PROFIT AND LOSS ACCOUNT

	£	£
Sales		12,500
Cost of sales (= purchases in this case)		(5,000)
Gross profit		7,500
Expenses		
Rent	3,500	
Bank loan interest	100	
Other expenses	1,900	
		(5,500)
Net profit		2,000

The balance sheet

1.19 Look back at the ledger accounts of R Kala. Now that we have dealt with those relating to income and expenses, which ones are left? The answer is that we still have to find out what to do with cash, capital, bank loan, trade creditors, shop fittings, debtors and the drawings account.

1.20 Are these the only ledger accounts left? No: don't forget there is still the last one we opened up, called the trading, profit and loss account. The balance on this account represents the *profit* earned by the business, and if you go through the arithmetic, you will find that it has a credit balance, a profit, of £2,000. (Not surprisingly, this is the figure that is shown in the trading, profit and loss account financial statement.)

1.21 These remaining accounts must also be balanced and ruled off, but since they represent assets and liabilities of the business (not income and expenses) their balances are not transferred to the trading profit and loss account. Instead they are *carried down* in the books of the business. This means that they become opening balances for the next accounting period and indicate the value of the assets and liabilities at the end of one period and the beginning of the next.

1.22 The conventional method of ruling off a ledger account at the end of an accounting period is illustrated by the bank loan account in R Kala's books:

BANK LOAN ACCOUNT

	£		£
Balance carried down (c/d)	1,000	Cash (D)	1,000
		Balance brought down (b/d)	1,000

1.23 R Kala therefore begins the new accounting period with a credit balance of £1,000 on this account. A *credit balance* brought down is a liability. An asset would be represented by a *debit balance* brought down.

1.24 One further point is worth noting before we move on to complete this example. You will remember that a proprietor's capital comprises any cash introduced by him, plus any profits made by the business, less any drawings made by him. At the stage we have now reached these three elements are contained in different ledger accounts: cash introduced of £7,000 appears in the capital account; drawings of £1,500 appear in the drawings account; and the profit made by the business is represented by the £2,000 credit balance on the trading profit and loss account. It is convenient to gather together all these amounts into one capital account, in the same way as we earlier gathered together income and expense accounts into one trading and profit and loss account.

1.25 If we go ahead and gather the three amounts together, the results are as follows.

DRAWINGS

	£		£
Cash	1,500	Capital a/c	1,500

TRADING, PROFIT AND LOSS ACCOUNT

	£		£
Purchases	5,000	Sales	12,500
Rent	3,500		
Bank loan interest	100		
Other expenses	1,900		
Capital a/c	2,000		
	12,500		12,500

CAPITAL

	£		£
Drawings	1,500	Cash	7,000
Balance c/d	7,500	Trading, P & L a/c	2,000
	9,000		9,000
		Balance b/d	7,500

1.26 A re-arrangement of these balances will complete R Kala's simple balance sheet.

R KALA
BALANCE SHEET AT END OF FIRST TRADING PERIOD

	£
Fixed assets	
Shop fittings	2,000
Current assets	
Cash	6,500
Total assets	8,500
Liabilities	
Bank loan	(1,000)
Net assets	7,500
Proprietor's capital	7,500

1.27 For limited companies, when a balance sheet is drawn up for an accounting period which is not the first one, then it ought to show the capital at the start of the accounting period and the capital at the end of the accounting period. This is illustrated in the following example.

Example: From ledger accounts to financial statements

1.28 A business is established with capital of £2,000, and this amount is paid into a business bank account by the proprietor. During the first year's trading, the following transactions occurred.

	£
Purchases of goods for resale, on credit	4,300
Payments to trade creditors	3,600
Sales, all on credit	5,800
Payments from debtors	3,200
Fixed assets purchased for cash	1,500
Other expenses, all paid in cash	900

The bank has provided an overdraft facility of up to £3,000.

Prepare the ledger accounts, a trading, profit and loss account for the year and a balance sheet as at the end of the year.

Solution: From trial balance to financial statements

1.29 The first thing to do is to open ledger accounts so that the transactions can be entered up. The relevant accounts which we need for this example are: cash; capital; trade creditors; purchases; fixed assets; sales and debtors.

1.30 The next step is to work out the double entry bookkeeping for each transaction. Normally you would write them straight into the accounts, but to make this example easier to follow, they are first listed below.

(a)	Establishing business (£2,000)	DR	Cash	CR	Capital
(b)	Purchases (£4,300)	DR	Purchases	CR	Creditors
(c)	Payments to creditors (£3,600)	DR	Creditors	CR	Cash
(d)	Sales (£5,800)	DR	Debtors	CR	Sales
(e)	Payments by debtors (£3,200)	DR	Cash	CR	Debtors
(f)	Fixed assets (£1,500)	DR	Fixed assets	CR	Cash
(g)	Other (cash) expenses (£900)	DR	Other expenses	CR	Cash

So far, the ledger accounts will look like this.

CASH
	£		£
Capital	2,000	Creditors	3,600
		Fixed assets	1,500
Debtors	3,200	Other expenses	900

CAPITAL
	£		£
		Cash	2,000

CREDITORS
	£		£
Cash	3,600	Purchases	4,300

PURCHASES
	£		£
Creditors	4,300		

FIXED ASSETS
	£		£
Cash	1,500		

SALES
	£		£
		Debtors	5,800

DEBTORS
	£		£
Sales	5,800	Cash	3,200

OTHER EXPENSES
	£		£
Cash	900		

1.31 The next thing to do is to balance all these accounts. It is at this stage that you could, if you wanted to, draw up a trial balance to make sure the double entries are accurate. There is not very much point in this simple example, but if you did draw up a trial balance, it would look like this.

		Debit £	Credit £
Cash			800
Capital			2,000
Creditors			700
Purchases		4,300	
Fixed assets		1,500	
Sales			5,800
Debtors		2,600	
Other expenses		900	
		9,300	9,300

1.32 After balancing the accounts, the trading, profit and loss account should be opened. Into it should be transferred all the balances relating to income and expenses (ie purchases, other expenses, and sales). At this point, the ledger accounts will be:

CASH

	£		£
Capital	2,000	Trade creditors	3,600
Debtors	3,200	Fixed assets	1,500
Balance c/d	800	Other expenses	900
	6,000		6,000
		Balance b/d	800*

* A credit balance b/d means that this cash item is a liability, not an asset. This indicates a bank overdraft of £800, with cash income of £5,200 falling short of payments of £6,000 by this amount.

CAPITAL

	£		£
Balance c/d	2,600	Cash	2,000
		P & L a/c	600
	2,600		2,600

TRADE CREDITORS

	£		£
Cash	3,600	Stores (purchases)	4,300
Balance c/d	700		
	4,300		4,300
		Balance b/d	700

PURCHASES ACCOUNT

	£		£
Trade creditors	4,300	Trading a/c	4,300

FIXED ASSETS

	£		£
Cash	1,500	Balance c/d	1,500
Balance b/d	1,500		

SALES

	£		£
Trading a/c	5,800		5,800

DEBTORS

	£		£
Sales	5,800	Cash	3,200
		Balance c/d	2,600
	5,800		5,800
Balance b/d	2,600		

OTHER EXPENSES

	£		£
Cash	900	P & L a/c	900

TRADING, PROFIT AND LOSS ACCOUNT

	£		£
Purchases account	4,300	Sales	5,800
Gross profit c/d	1,500		
	5,800		5,800
Other expenses	900	Gross profit b/d	1,500
Net profit (transferred to			
capital account)	600		
	1,500		1,500

1.33 So the trading, profit and loss account financial statement will be as follows.

TRADING, PROFIT AND LOSS ACCOUNT
FOR THE ACCOUNTING PERIOD

	£
Sales	5,800
Cost of sales (purchases)	(4,300)
Gross profit	1,500
Expenses	900
Net profit	600

1.34 Listing and then rearranging the balances on the ledger accounts gives the balance sheet as follows.

BALANCE SHEET AS AT THE END OF THE PERIOD

	£	£
Fixed assets		1,500
Current assets		
Debtors	2,600	
Current liabilities		
Bank overdraft	800	
Trade creditors	700	
	1,500	
Net current assets		1,100
		2,600
Capital		
At start of period		2,000
Net profit for period		600
At end of period		2,600

2 SUSPENSE ACCOUNTS

Centrally assessed 6/94, 12/94, 6/95

2.1 We must now look more closely at the best method of dealing with errors on a trial balance: the use of a suspense account. A suspense account is a *temporary* account which can be opened for a number of reasons. The most common reasons are:

(a) a trial balance is drawn up which does not balance (total debits do not equal total credits);

(b) the bookkeeper of a business knows where to post the credit side of a transaction, but does not know where to post the debit (or vice versa). For example, a cash payment might be made and must obviously be credited to cash. But the bookkeeper may not know what the payment is for, and so will not know which account to debit.

2.2 In both these cases, a temporary suspense account is opened up until the problem is sorted out. The next few paragraphs explain exactly how this works.

Use of suspense account: when the trial balance does not balance

2.3 When an error has occurred which results in an imbalance between total debits and total credits in the ledger accounts, the first step is to open a suspense account. For example, suppose an accountant draws up a trial balance and finds that, for some reason he cannot immediately discover, total debits exceed total credits by £162.

2.4 He knows that there is an error somewhere, but for the time being he opens a suspense account and enters a credit of £162 in it. This serves two purposes.

(a) Because the suspense account now exists, the accountant will not forget that there is an error (of £162) to be sorted out.

(b) Now that there is a credit of £162 in the suspense account, the trial balance balances.

2.5 When the cause of the £162 discrepancy is tracked down, it is corrected by means of a journal entry. For example, suppose it turned out that the accountant had accidentally failed to make a credit of £162 to purchases. The journal entry would be:

DEBIT	Suspense a/c	£162
CREDIT	Purchases	£162

To close off suspense a/c and correct error

2.6 Whenever an error occurs which results in total debits not being equal to total credits, the first step an accountant makes is to open up a suspense account. Three more examples are given below.

Example: Transposition error

2.7 The bookkeeper of Mixem Ltd made a transposition error when entering an amount for sales in the sales account. Instead of entering the correct amount of £37,453.60 he entered £37,543.60, transposing the 4 and 5. The debtors were posted correctly, and so when total debits and credits on the ledger accounts were compared, it was found that credits exceeded debits by £(37,543.60 – 37,453.60) = £90.

2.8 The initial step is to equalise the total debits and credits by posting a debit of £90 to a suspense account.

2.9 When the cause of the error is discovered, the double entry to correct it should be logged in the journal as:

DEBIT	Sales	£90
CREDIT	Suspense a/c	£90

To close off suspense a/c and correct transposition error

Example: Error of omission

2.10 When Snipe Builders paid the monthly salary cheques to its office staff, the payment of £5,250 was correctly entered in the cash account, but the bookkeeper omitted to debit the office salaries account. As a consequence, the total debit and credit balances on the ledger accounts were not equal, and credits exceeded debits by £5,250.

2.11 The initial step in correcting the situation is to debit £5,250 to a suspense account, to equalise the total debits and total credits.

2.12   When the cause of the error is discovered, the double entry to correct it should be logged in the journal as:

DEBIT   Office salaries account   £5,250
CREDIT   Suspense account   £5,250
To close off suspense account and correct error of omission

Example: Error of commission

2.13   A bookkeeper might make a mistake by entering what should be a debit entry as a credit, or vice versa. For example, suppose that a credit customer pays £460 of the £660 he owes to Ashdown Tree Felling Contractors, but Ashdown's bookkeeper has *debited* £460 on the debtors account in the nominal ledger by mistake instead of crediting the payment received.

2.14   The total debit balances in Ashdown's ledger accounts would now exceed the total credits by 2 × £460 = £920. The initial step in correcting the error would be to make a credit entry of £920 in a suspense account. When the cause of the error is discovered, it should be corrected as follows.

DEBIT   Suspense account   £920
CREDIT   Debtors   £920
To close off suspense account and correct error of commission

2.15   In the debtors account in the nominal ledger, the correction would appear therefore as follows.

DEBTORS ACCOUNT

	£		£
Balance b/f	660	Suspense account (error corrected)	920
Cash (payment incorrectly		Balance c/f	200
debited)	460		
	1,120		1,120

Use of suspense account: not knowing where to post a transaction

2.16   Another use of suspense accounts occurs when a bookkeeper does not know in which account to post one side of a transaction. Until the mystery is sorted out, the credit entry can be recorded in a suspense account. A typical example is when the business receives cash through the post from a source which cannot be determined. The double entry in the accounts would be a debit in the cash book and a credit to a suspense account.

2.17   Similarly, when the bookkeeper knows in which account to make one entry, but for some reason does not know where to make the corresponding entry, this can be posted to a suspense account. A very common example is to credit proceeds on disposal of fixed assets to the suspense account instead of working out the profit or loss on disposal.

Example: Not knowing where to post a transaction

2.18   Windfall Garments received a cheque in the post for £620. The name on the cheque is R J Beasley, but Windfall Garments have no idea who this person is, nor why he should be sending £620. The bookkeeper decides to open a suspense account, so that the double entry for the transaction is:

DEBIT   Cash   £620
CREDIT   Suspense account   £620

2.19 Eventually, it transpires that the cheque was in payment for a debt owed by the Haute Couture Corner Shop and paid out of the proprietor's (Mr Beasley's) personal bank account. The suspense account can now be cleared, as follows.

DEBIT	Suspense account	£620
CREDIT	Debtors	£620

Suspense accounts might contain several items

2.20 If more than one error or unidentifiable posting to a ledger account arises during an accounting period, they will all be merged together in the same suspense account. Indeed, until the causes of the errors are discovered, the bookkeepers are unlikely to know exactly how many errors there are. A central or devolved assessment task might give you a balance on a suspense account, together with enough information to make the necessary corrections, leaving a nil balance on the suspense account and correct balances on various other accounts. In practice, of course, finding these errors is far from easy!

Suspense accounts are temporary

2.21 It must be stressed that a suspense account can only be *temporary*. Postings to a suspense account are only made when the bookkeeper does not know yet what to do, or when an error has occurred. Mysteries must be solved, and errors must be corrected. Under no circumstances should there still be a suspense account when it comes to preparing the balance sheet of a business. The suspense account must be cleared and all the correcting entries made before the final accounts are drawn up.

3 COST OF GOODS SOLD

3.1 Before we look at the problems surrounding incomplete records in Chapter 8, there is an important area we need to examine which has a direct bearing on the preparation of accounts: *stocks*. The valuation of stock is important as it directly affects gross profit, as we will see in Section 6 of this chapter. It also has an impact on the current assets in the balance sheet. Stock valuation rules are embodied in SSAP 9 *Stocks and long-term contracts*. (You should note that long-term contracts are not studied at the AAT Intermediate stage.)

3.2 When we looked at the trading, profit and loss account near the beginning of this Text, we defined profit as the value of sales less the cost of sales and expenses. This definition might seem simple enough; however, it is not always immediately clear how much the cost of sales or expenses are. A variety of difficulties can arise in measuring them: some of these problems can be dealt with fairly easily, whereas others are less obvious to solve. The purpose of the rest of this chapter is to describe some of these problems and their solutions.

Unsold goods in stock at the end of an accounting period

3.3 Goods might be unsold at the end of an accounting period and so still be held in stock at the end of the period. The purchase cost of these goods should *not* be included therefore in the cost of sales of the period.

Example: Closing stock

3.4 Suppose that Perry P Louis, trading as the Umbrella Shop, ends his financial year on 30 September each year. On 1 October 19X4 he had no goods in stock. During the year to 30 September 19X5, he purchased 30,000 umbrellas costing £60,000 from umbrella wholesalers and suppliers. He resold the umbrellas for £5 each, and sales for the year amounted to £100,000 (20,000 umbrellas). At 30 September there were 10,000 unsold umbrellas left in stock, valued at £2 each.

What was Perry P Louis's gross profit for the year?

Solution: Closing stock

3.5 Perry P Louis purchased 30,000 umbrellas, but only sold 20,000. Purchase costs of £60,000 and sales of £100,000 do not represent the same quantity of goods.

The gross profit for the year should be calculated by 'matching' the sales value of the 20,000 umbrellas sold with the cost of those 20,000 umbrellas. The cost of sales in this example is therefore the cost of purchases minus the cost of goods in stock at the year end.

	£	£
Sales (20,000 units)		100,000
Purchases (30,000 units)	60,000	
Less closing stock (10,000 units @ £2)	20,000	
Cost of sales (20,000 units)		40,000
Gross profit		60,000

Example continued

3.6 We shall continue the example of the Umbrella Shop into its next accounting year, 1 October 19X5 to 30 September 19X6. Suppose that during the course of this year, Perry P Louis purchased 40,000 umbrellas at a total cost of £95,000. During the year he sold 45,000 umbrellas for £230,000. At 30 September 19X6 he had 5,000 umbrellas left in stock, which had cost £12,000.

What was his gross profit for the year?

Solution continued

3.7 In this accounting year, he purchased 40,000 umbrellas to add to the 10,000 he already had in stock at the start of the year. He sold 45,000, leaving 5,000 umbrellas in stock at the year end. Once again, gross profit should be calculated by matching the value of 45,000 units of sales with the cost of those 45,000 units.

The cost of sales is the value of the 10,000 umbrellas in stock at the beginning of the year, plus the cost of the 40,000 umbrellas purchased, less the value of the 5,000 umbrellas in stock at the year end.

	£	£
Sales (45,000 units)		230,000
Opening stock (10,000 units) *	20,000	
Add purchases (40,000 units)	95,000	
	115,000	
Less closing stock (5,000 units)	12,000	
Cost of sales (45,000 units)		103,000
Gross profit		127,000

*Taken from the closing stock value of the previous accounting year, see Paragraph 3.5.

The cost of goods sold

3.8 The cost of goods sold is found by applying the following formula.

	£
Opening stock value	X
Add cost of purchases (or, in the case of a manufacturing company, the cost of production)	X
	X
Less closing stock value	(X)
Equals cost of goods sold	X

In other words, to match 'sales' and the 'cost of goods sold', it is necessary to adjust the cost of goods manufactured or purchased to allow for increases or reduction in stock levels during the period.

Example: Cost of goods sold

3.9 On 1 January 19X6, the Grand Union Food Stores had goods in stock valued at £6,000. During 19X6 its proprietor, who ran the shop, purchased supplies costing £50,000. Sales turnover for the year to 31 December 19X6 amounted to £80,000. The cost of goods in stock at 31 December 19X6 was £12,500.

Task

Calculate the gross profit for the year.

Solution: Cost of goods sold

3.10 GRAND UNION FOOD STORES
TRADING ACCOUNT FOR THE YEAR ENDED 31 DECEMBER 19X6

	£	£
Sales		80,000
Opening stocks	6,000	
Add purchases	50,000	
	56,000	
Less closing stocks	12,500	
Cost of goods sold		43,500
Gross profit		36,500

The cost of carriage inwards and outwards
Centrally assessed 6/94

3.11 'Carriage' refers to the cost of transporting purchased goods from the supplier to the premises of the business which has bought them. Someone has to pay for these delivery costs: sometimes the supplier pays, and sometimes the purchaser pays. When the purchaser pays, the cost to the purchaser is *carriage inwards*. When the supplier pays, the cost to the supplier is known as *carriage outwards*.

3.12 The cost of *carriage inwards* is usually added to the cost of purchases, and is therefore included in the trading account.

The cost of *carriage outwards* is a selling and distribution expense in the profit and loss account.

Example: Carriage inwards and carriage outwards

3.13 Gwyn Tring, trading as Clickety Clocks, imports and resells cuckoo clocks and grandfather clocks. He must pay for the costs of delivering the clocks from his supplier in Switzerland to his shop in Wales. He resells the clocks to other traders throughout the country, paying the costs of carriage for the consignments from his business premises to his customers.

On 1 July 19X5, he had clocks in stock valued at £17,000. During the year to 30 June 19X6 he purchased more clocks at a cost of £75,000. Carriage inwards amounted to £2,000. Sales for the year were £162,100. Other expenses of the business amounted to £56,000 excluding carriage outwards which cost £2,500. Gwyn Tring took drawings of £20,000 from the business during the course of the year. The value of the goods in stock at the year end was £15,400.

Task

Prepare the trading, profit and loss account of Clickety Clocks for the year ended 30 June 19X6.

Solution: Carriage inwards and carriage outwards

3.14 CLICKETY CLOCKS
TRADING, PROFIT AND LOSS ACCOUNT
FOR THE YEAR ENDED 30 JUNE 19X6

	£	£
Sales		162,100
Opening stock	17,000	
Purchases	75,000	
Carriage inwards	2,000	
	94,000	
Less closing stock	15,400	
Cost of goods sold		78,600
Gross profit		83,500
Carriage outwards	2,500	
Other expenses	56,000	
		58,500
Net profit (transferred to balance sheet)		25,000

Goods written off or written down
Centrally assessed 6/94 - 6/97

3.15 A trader might be *unable to sell* all the goods that he purchases, because a number of things might happen to the goods before they can be sold. For example:

(a) goods might be lost or stolen;

(b) goods might be damaged, and so become worthless. Such damaged goods might be thrown away;

(c) goods might become obsolete or out of fashion. These might have to be thrown away, or possibly sold off at a very low price in a clearance sale.

3.16 When goods are lost, stolen or thrown away as worthless, the business will make a loss on those goods because their 'sales value' will be nil.

Similarly, when goods lose value because they have become obsolete or out of fashion, the business will make a loss if their clearance sales value is less than their cost. For example, if goods which originally cost £500 are now obsolete and could only be sold for £150, the business would suffer a loss of £350.

3.17 If, at the end of an accounting period, a business still has goods in stock which are either worthless or worth less than their original cost, the value of the stocks should be written down to:

(a) nothing if they are worthless; or
(b) their *net realisable value* if this is less than their original cost.

This means that the loss will be reported as soon as the loss is foreseen, even if the goods have not yet been thrown away or sold off at a cheap price. This is an application of the *prudence concept*.

3.18 The costs of stock written off or written down should not usually cause any problems in calculating the gross profit of a business, because the cost of goods sold will include the cost of stocks written off or written down, as the following example shows.

Example: Stocks written off and written down

3.19 Lucas Wagg, trading as Fairlock Fashions, ends his financial year on 31 March. At 1 April 19X5 he had goods in stock valued at £8,800. During the year to 31 March 19X6, he purchased goods costing £48,000. Fashion goods which cost £2,100 were still held in stock at 31 March 19X6, and Lucas Wagg believes that these could only now be sold at a sale price of £400. The goods still held in stock at 31 March 19X6 (including the fashion goods) had an original purchase cost of £7,600. Sales for the year were £81,400.

Task

Calculate the gross profit of Fairlock Fashions for the year ended 31 March 19X6.

Solution: Stocks written off and written down

3.20 The initial calculation of closing stock values is as follows.

STOCK COUNT

	At cost £	Revalued amount £	Amount written down £
Fashion goods	2,100	400	1,700
Other goods	5,500	5,500	-
	7,600	5,900	1,700

FAIRLOCK FASHIONS
TRADING ACCOUNT FOR THE YEAR ENDED 31 MARCH 19X6

	£	£
Sales		81,400
Value of opening stock	8,800	
Purchases	48,000	
	56,800	
Less closing stock	5,900	
Cost of goods sold		50,900
Gross profit		30,500

3.21 You should see that the write off of £1,700 is *automatic* because the closing stock deducted from cost of sales is £1,700 less than it would have been if valued at cost; cost of sales is therefore £1,700 higher than it would have been without the write down of stock.

4 ACCOUNTING FOR OPENING AND CLOSING STOCKS
Centrally assessed 6/94 - 6/97

4.1 We have now seen that in order to calculate gross profit it is necessary to work out the cost of goods sold, and in order to calculate the cost of goods sold it is necessary to have values for the *opening stock* (stock in hand at the beginning of the accounting period) and *closing stock* (stock in hand at the end of the accounting period). In other words, the trading part of a profit and loss account includes:

	£
Opening stock	X
Plus purchases	X
Less closing stock	(X)
Equals cost of goods sold	X

4.2 However, just writing down this formula hides three problems.

(a) How do you manage to get a precise *count* of stock in hand at any one time?

(b) Even once it has been counted, how do you *value* the stock?

(c) Assuming the stock is given a value, how does the *double entry* bookkeeping for stock work?

Let us look at (c) first.

Ledger accounting for stocks

4.3 It has already been shown that purchases are introduced to the trading account by means of the double entry:

DEBIT	Trading account	£X
CREDIT	Purchases account	£X

4.4 But what about opening and closing stocks? How are their values accounted for in the double entry bookkeeping system? The answer is that a *stock account* must be kept. *This stock account is only ever used at the end of an accounting period, when the business counts up and values the stock in hand*, in a stocktake.

(a) When a stocktake is made, the business will have a value for its closing stock, and the double entry is:

DEBIT	Stock account (closing stock value)	£X
CREDIT	Trading account	£X

However, rather than show the closing stock as a 'plus' value in the trading account (say by adding it to sales) it is usual to show it as a 'minus' figure in arriving at cost of sales. This is illustrated in Paragraph 4.1 above. The debit balance on stock account represents an asset, which will be shown as part of current assets in the balance sheet.

(b) Closing stock at the end of one period becomes opening stock at the start of the next period. The stock account remains unchanged until the end of the next period, when the value of opening stock is taken to the trading account.

DEBIT	Trading account	£X
CREDIT	Stock account (value of opening stock)	£X

Example: Ledger accounting for stock

4.5 This example is very similar to the example in Paragraphs 1.28 to 1.34 above, but with some variations. A business is established with capital of £2,000 and this amount is paid into a business bank account by the proprietor. During the first year's trading, the following transactions occurred.

	£
Purchases of goods for resale, on credit	4,300
Payments to trade creditors	3,600
Sales, all on credit	4,000
Payments from debtors	3,200
Fixed assets purchased for cash	1,500
Other expenses, all paid in cash	900

The bank has provided an overdraft facility of up to £3,000. All 'other expenses' relate to the current year.

Closing stocks of goods are valued at £1,800. (Because this is the first year of the business, there are no opening stocks.)

Ignore depreciation and drawings.

Task

Prepare the ledger accounts and a trading, profit and loss account for the year.

Solution: Ledger accounting for stock

4.6   CASH

	£		£
Capital	2,000	Trade creditors	3,600
Debtors	3,200	Fixed assets	1,500
Balance c/d	800	Other expenses	900
	6,000		6,000
		Balance b/d	800

CAPITAL

	£		£
Balance c/d	2,600	Cash	2,000
		P & L a/c	600
	2,600		2,600
		Balance b/d	2,600

TRADE CREDITORS

	£		£
Cash	3,600	Purchases	4,300
Balance c/d	700		
	4,300		4,300
		Balance b/d	700

PURCHASES ACCOUNT

	£		£
Trade creditors	4,300	Trading a/c	4,300

FIXED ASSETS

	£		£
Cash	1,500	Balance c/d	1,500
Balance b/d	1,500		

SALES

	£		£
Trading a/c	4,000	Debtors	4,000

DEBTORS

	£		£
Sales	4,000	Cash	3,200
		Balance c/d	800
	4,000		4,000
Balance b/d	800		

OTHER EXPENSES

	£		£
Cash	900	P & L a/c	900

TRADING, PROFIT AND LOSS ACCOUNT

	£		£
Purchases account	4,300	Sales	4,000
Gross profit c/d	1,500	Closing stock (stock account)	1,800
	5,800		5,800
Other expenses	900	Gross profit b/d	1,500
Net profit (transferred to capital account)	600		
	1,500		1,500

Alternatively, closing stock could be shown as a minus value on the debit side of the trading account, instead of a credit entry, giving purchases £4,300 less closing stock £1,800 equals cost of goods sold £2,500.

STOCK ACCOUNT

	£
Trading account (closing stock)	1,800

This will be the opening stock of the new period.

4.7 Make sure you can see what has happened here. The balance on the stock account was £1,800, which appears in the balance sheet as a current asset. As it happens, the £1,800 closing stock was the only entry in the stock account: there was no figure for opening stock.

If there had been, it would have been eliminated by transferring it as a debit balance to the trading account:

CREDIT   Stock account (with value of opening stock)
DEBIT   Trading account (with value of opening stock)

The debit in the trading account would then have increased the cost of sales, ie opening stock is added to purchases in calculating cost of sales. Again, this is illustrated in Paragraph 4.1 above.

4.8 So if we can establish the value of stocks on hand, the above paragraphs and example show us how to account for that value. That takes care of one of the problems noted in the introduction of this section. But now another of those problems becomes apparent: how do we establish the value of stocks on hand? The first step must be to establish *how much* stock is held.

4.9 Note that stocks sent to customers on a *sale or return* basis should be *included* in closing stock if the customer still has not sold them at the year end. This means that no accounting entries should be made until the stock is sold by the customer.

5   STOCKTAKING AND STOCK ACCRUALS

5.1 Business trading is a continuous activity, but accounting statements must be drawn up at a particular date. In preparing a balance sheet it is necessary to 'freeze' the activity of a business so as to determine its assets and liabilities at a given moment. This includes establishing the quantities of stocks on hand, which can create problems.

5.2 A business buys stocks continually during its trading operations and either sells the goods onwards to customers or incorporates them as raw materials in manufactured products. This constant movement of stocks makes it difficult to establish what exactly is held at any precise moment.

5.3 In simple cases, when a business holds easily counted and relatively small amounts of stock, quantities of stocks on hand at the balance sheet date can be determined by *physically counting* them in a stocktake.

5.4 The continuous nature of trading activity may cause a problem in that stock movements will not necessarily cease during the time that the physical stocktake is in progress. Two possible solutions are:

(a) to close down the business while the count takes place; or
(b) to keep detailed records of stock movements during the course of the stocktake.

5.5 Closing down the business for a short period for a stocktake (say over a weekend or at Christmas) is considerably easier than trying to keep detailed records of stock movements during a stocktake. So most businesses prefer that method unless they happen to keep detailed records of stock movements anyway (eg because they wish to keep strict control on stock movements).

5.6 In more complicated cases, where a business holds considerable quantities of varied stock, an alternative approach to establishing stock quantities is to maintain continuous stock records. This means that a card is kept for every item of stock, showing receipts and issues from the stores, and a running total. (Alternatively, the records may be computerised - quite likely in a large company.) A few stock items are counted each day to make sure their record cards are correct. This is called a 'continuous' stocktake because it is spread out over the year rather than completed in one stocktake at a designated time.

Stock accruals

5.7 In Chapter 6 we looked at accruals and we mentioned *purchase accruals* (which are sometimes called *stock accruals*). These arise where goods have been received before the year end and included in stock, but no invoice has yet been received. Without an invoice, it will not have been possible to record the liability to the supplier. It is therefore necessary to determine those items of stock which have not been recorded as a liability.

5.8 The procedure for determining those items of stock for which no liability has been recorded is as follows.

(a) Match all invoices and Goods Received Notes (GRNs) received in the last month of the year.

(b) All unmatched GRNs should be listed.

(c) The stock on the GRNs must be costed at its purchase price. Delivery notes (which should be kept with the GRNs) received from suppliers will sometimes show the prices of the items of stock delivered. Where this is not the case, it will be necessary to price the stock using current order forms or pricing lists.

Example: Stock accruals

5.9 The following GRNs are found to be unmatched with invoices at the year end (31 December 19X3).

ORDRAM QUICK
GOODS RECEIVED NOTE

No. G924
Date: 26 December 19X3

Item	Code	Quantity	P.O. No.
Onyxel Grade B	0048	200m²	1233
Trilam 22	7050	180m²	1233
Trilam 24	7060	200m²	1241

Comments

ORDRAM QUICK
GOODS RECEIVED NOTE

No. G977
Date: 27 December 19X3

Item	Code	Quantity	P.O. No.
Enlam 20 – polar white	9248	250m²	1233
Enlam 25 – polar white	9252	300m²	1233

Comments

ORDRAM QUICK GOODS RECEIVED NOTE		No. H010 Date: *29 December 19X3*	
Item	Code	Quantity	P.O. No.
Plymel 30	*1041*	*150m²*	*1274*
Onyxel Grade B	*0048*	*200m²*	*1233*
Comments			

The current pricing list includes the following.

Product	*Price/ms* £
Enlam 20	0.85
Enlam 25	0.90
Onyxel Grade B	0.45
Plymel 30	1.05
Trilam 22	1.21
Trilam 24	2.11

Task

List and price the unmatched GRNs at the year end.

Solution: Stock accruals

5.10 *GRN*

	£
G924 (200 × £0.45) + (180 × £1.21) + (200 × £2.11)	729.80
G997 (250 × £0.85) + (300 × £0.90)	482.50
H010 (150 × £1.05) + (200 × £0.45)	247.50
	1,459.80

5.11 One obstacle is overcome once a business has established how much stock is on hand. But another of the problems noted earlier immediately arises. What value should the business place on those stocks? SSAP 9 *Stocks and long-term contracts* contains the rules governing the valuation of stock.

6 VALUING STOCKS
Centrally assessed 6/94 - 6/97

6.1 There are several methods which, in theory, might be used for the valuation of stock items.

(a) Stocks might be valued at their expected *selling price*.

(b) Stocks might be valued at their expected selling price, less any costs still to be incurred in getting them ready for sale and then selling them. This amount is referred to as the *net realisable value* (NRV) of the stocks.

(c) Stocks might be valued at their *historical cost* (the cost at which they were originally bought).

(d) Stocks might be valued at the amount it would cost to replace them. This amount is referred to as the *current replacement cost* of stocks.

6.2 Current replacement costs are not used in the type of accounts dealt with in this Text, and so are not considered further.

6.3 The use of *selling prices* in stock valuation is ruled out because this would create a profit for the business before the stock has been sold.

6.4 A simple example might help to explain this. Suppose that a trader buys two items of stock, each costing £100. He can sell them for £140 each, but in the accounting period we shall consider, he has only sold one of them. The other is closing stock in hand.

6.5 Since only one item has been sold, you might think it is common sense that profit ought to be £40. But if closing stock is valued at selling price, profit would be £80 as profit would be taken on the closing stock as well.

	£	£
Sales		140
Opening stock	-	
Purchases (2 × 100)	200	
	200	
Less closing stock (at selling price)	140	
Cost of sale		60
Profit		80

This would contradict the accounting concept of *prudence*, as it involves claiming a profit before the item has actually been sold.

6.6 The same objection *usually* applies to the use of *net realisable value (NRV)* in stock valuation. Say that the item purchased for £100 requires £5 of further expenditure in getting it ready for sale and then selling it (for example £5 of processing costs and distribution costs). If its expected selling price is £140, its NRV is £(140 – 5) = £135. To value it at £135 in the balance sheet would still be to anticipate a profit of £35.

6.7 We are left with *historical cost* as the normal basis of stock valuation. The only times when historical cost is not used is in the exceptional cases when the prudence concept requires a lower value to be used.

6.8 Staying with the example in Paragraph 6.6, suppose that the market in this kind of product suddenly slumps and the item's expected selling price is only £90. The item's NRV is then £(90 – 5) = £85 and the business has in effect made a loss of £15 (£100 – £85). The prudence concept requires that losses should be recognised as soon as they are foreseen. This can be achieved by valuing the stock item in the balance sheet at its NRV of £85.

6.9 The argument developed above suggests that the rule to follow is that stocks should be valued at cost, or if lower, net realisable value. SSAP 9 *Stocks and long-term contracts* states that stock *should be valued at the lower of cost and net realisable value.* This is an important rule and one which you should learn by heart.

Applying the basic valuation rule

6.10 If a business has many stock items on hand, the comparison of cost and NRV should theoretically be carried out for each item separately. It is not sufficient to compare the total cost of all stock items with their total NRV. An example will show why.

6.11 Suppose a company has four items of stock on hand at the end of its accounting period. Their cost and NRVs are as follows.

Stock item	Cost	NRV	Lower of cost/NRV
	£	£	£
1	27	32	27
2	14	8	8
3	43	55	43
4	29	40	29
	113	135	107

6.12 It would be incorrect to compare total costs (£113) with total NRV (£135) and to state stocks at £113 in the balance sheet. The company can foresee a loss of £6 on item 2 and this should be recognised. If the four items are taken together in total the loss on item 2 is masked by the anticipated profits on the other items. By performing the cost/NRV comparison for each item separately, the prudent valuation of £107 can be derived. This is the value which should appear in the balance sheet. This is an example of the fifth accounting principle introduced by the Companies Act 1985 and mentioned in Chapter 5: the *separate valuation principle*.

6.13 However, for a company with large amounts of stock this procedure may be impracticable. In this case it is acceptable to group *similar* items into categories and perform the comparison of cost and NRV category by category, rather than item by item.

6.14 So have we now solved the problem of how a business should value its stocks? It seems that all the business has to do is to choose the lower of cost and net realisable value. This is true as far as it goes, but there is one further problem, perhaps not so easy to foresee: for a given item of stock, what was the cost?

Determining the purchase cost

6.15 Stock may be raw materials or components bought from suppliers, finished goods which have been made by the business but not yet sold, or work in the process of production, but only part-completed (this type of stock is called work in progress or WIP). It will simplify matters, however, if we think about the historical cost of purchased raw materials and components, which ought to be their *purchase price*.

6.16 A business may be continually purchasing consignments of a particular component. As each consignment is received from suppliers they are stored in the appropriate bin or on the appropriate shelf or pallet, where they will be mingled with previous consignments. When the storekeeper issues components to production he will simply pull out from the bin the nearest components to hand, which may have arrived in the latest consignment or in an earlier consignment or in several different consignments. However, the price paid for the same component will change over time; our concern is to devise a pricing technique, a rule of thumb which we can use to attribute a cost to each of the components issued from stores.

6.17 There are several techniques which are used in practice.

(a) *FIFO (first in, first out)*. Using this technique, we assume that components are used in the order in which they are received from suppliers. The components issued are deemed to have formed part of the oldest consignment still unused and are costed accordingly.

(b) *LIFO (last in, first out)*. This involves the opposite assumption, that components issued to production originally formed part of the most recent delivery, while older consignments lie in the bin undisturbed.

(c) *Average cost*. As purchase prices change with each new consignment, the average price of components in the bin is constantly changed. Each component in the bin at any moment is assumed to have been purchased at the average price of all components in the bin at that moment.

(d) *Standard cost.* A pre-determined standard cost is applied to all stock items. If this standard price differs from prices actually paid during the period it will be necessary to write off the difference as a 'variance' in the profit and loss account.

(e) *Replacement cost.* The arbitrary assumption is made that the cost at which a stock unit was purchased is the amount it would cost to replace it. This is often (but not necessarily) the unit cost of stocks purchased in the next consignment *following* the issue of the component to production. For this reason, a method which produces similar results to replacement costs is called NIFO (next in, first out).

6.18 Any or all of these methods might provide a suitable basis for valuing stocks. But it is worth mentioning here that if you are preparing *financial* accounts you would normally expect to use FIFO or average costs for the balance sheet valuation of stock. SSAP 9 specifically discourages the use of LIFO and replacement costs because both may anticipate profits (against the prudence concept) in times of rising prices. Nevertheless, you should know about all of the methods so that you can discuss the differences between them. The calculation of stock values using these methods is covered in Unit 6 *Cost Accounting 1.*

Key points in this chapter

- To prepare a *trial balance*:

  o the ledger accounts must be *balanced* and *collected*;

  o the debits and credits must be *equal* and any inequality must be investigated and corrected;

  o a *trading, profit and loss account* must be created.

- A *profit and loss ledger account* is opened up to gather all items relating to income and expenses. When rearranged, the items make up the profit and loss account financial statement.

- The balances on all remaining ledger accounts (including the profit and loss account) can be listed and rearranged to form the *balance sheet*.

- The *cost of goods sold* is calculated by applying the formula:

	£
Opening stock value	X
Add cost of purchases or production	X
	X
Less closing stock value	(X)
Equals cost of goods sold	X

- A *stock ledger account* is kept which is only ever used at the end of an accounting period, when the business counts up and values stock in hand, in a *stocktake*.

- GRNs must be matched with invoices received just after the year end to identify *stock accruals*.

- There are various methods of determining the *cost* of stock: FIFO, average cost and standard cost are allowed by SSAP 9 but LIFO and replacement cost methods are discouraged.

For practice on the points covered in this chapter you should now attempt the Practice Exercises in Session 7 of the Financial Accounting Workbook

8 Incomplete records

This chapter covers the following topics.

1 **Preparing accounts from incomplete records**

2 **The opening balance sheet**

3 **Credit sales and debtors**

4 **Purchases and trade creditors**

5 **Purchases, stocks and cost of sales**

6 **The cash book**

7 **Accruals and prepayments**

8 **Drawings**

9 **Using simple accounting ratios**

10 **Comprehensive example**

1 PREPARING ACCOUNTS FROM INCOMPLETE RECORDS
Centrally assessed 6/94 - 6/97

1.1 Incomplete records problems occur when a business does not have a full set of accounting records. The problems can arise for two reasons.

(a) The proprietor of the business does not keep a full set of accounts.
(b) Some of the business accounts are accidentally lost or destroyed.

1.2 The problem is to prepare a set of year-end accounts for the business; a trading, profit and loss account, and a balance sheet. Since the business does not have a full set of accounts, preparing the final accounts is not a simple matter of closing off accounts and transferring balances to the trading, profit and loss account, or showing outstanding balances in the balance sheet. Preparing the final accounts involves the following tasks.

(a) Establishing the cost of purchases and other expenses

(b) Establishing the total amount of sales

(c) Establishing the amount of creditors, accruals, debtors and prepayments at the end of the year

1.3 Questions or assessment tasks often take incomplete records problems a stage further, by introducing an 'incident' such as fire or burglary which leaves the owner of the business uncertain about how much stock has been destroyed or stolen.

1.4 It is worth remembering that, in practice, when incomplete records situations arise and investigations are necessary, the Accounting Technician will need to question most of the accounting staff and examine their work. It is vital that tact and courtesy prevail in such situations, particularly as people will be very defensive if they feel that their work is being criticised. Blame should not be apportioned rashly when things go wrong, but only after careful consideration, and through the organisation's normal procedures. The staff you question will be far more cooperative if you are polite and understanding.

1.5 To understand what incomplete records are about, it will obviously be useful now to look at what exactly might be incomplete. We shall consider the following items in turn.

(a) The opening balance sheet
(b) Credit sales and debtors
(c) Purchases and trade creditors
(d) Purchases, stocks and the cost of sales
(e) Stolen goods or goods destroyed
(f) The cash book
(g) Accruals and prepayments
(h) Drawings (for a sole trader)

Note that there is *always* an incomplete records question as one section of the Central Assessment for these units. Each question uses a variety of the techniques and procedures discussed below, so they will not be highlighted separately as having arisen in a central assessment. This means that any other section of this chapter noted as centrally assessed has come up in *another section* of the central assessment.

2 THE OPENING BALANCE SHEET

2.1 In practice there should not be any missing item in the opening balance sheet of the business, because it should be available from the preparation of the previous year's final accounts. However, an examination problem might provide information about the assets and liabilities of the business at the beginning of the period under review, but then leave the balancing figure unspecified. This *balancing figure* represents the opening balance of the profit and loss account (or, in the case of a sole trader, the proprietor's business capital).

2.2 For example, a business has the following assets and liabilities as at 1 January 19X3.

	£
Fixtures and fittings at cost	7,000
Provision for depreciation, fixtures and fittings	4,000
Motor vehicles at cost	12,000
Provision for depreciation, motor vehicles	6,800
Stock in trade	4,500
Trade debtors	5,200
Cash at bank and in hand	1,230
Trade creditors	3,700
Prepayment	450
Accrued rent	2,000
Capital	1,000

The balance sheet of the business can be prepared and the balancing figure is the profit and loss account balance.

	£	£
Fixtures and fittings at cost	7,000	
Less accumulated depreciation	4,000	
		3,000
Motor vehicles at cost	12,000	
Less accumulated depreciation	6,800	
		5,200
		8,200
Current assets		
Stock in trade	4,500	
Trade debtors	5,200	
Prepayment	450	
Cash	1,230	
	11,380	
Current liabilities		
Trade creditors	3,700	
Accrual	2,000	
	5,700	
Net current assets		5,680
		13,880
Capital		
Capital		1,000
Profit and loss account (balancing figure)		12,880
		13,880

2.3 The opening balance sheet should now provide some of the information needed to prepare the final accounts for the current period.

3 CREDIT SALES AND DEBTORS

3.1 If a business does not keep a record of its sales on credit, the value of these sales can be derived from the opening balance of trade debtors, the closing balance of trade debtors, and the payments received from trade debtors during the period.

Credit sales are calculated as follows.

	£
Payments received from trade debtors	X
Plus closing balance of trade debtors (since these represent sales in the current period for which cash payment has not yet been received)	X
Less opening balance of trade debtors (unless these become bad debts, they will pay what they owe in the current period for sales in a previous period)	(X)
Credit sales during the period	X

3.2 For example, suppose that a business had trade debtors of £1,750 on 1 April 19X4 and trade debtors of £3,140 on 31 March 19X5. If payments received from trade debtors during the year to 31 March 19X5 were £28,490, and if there are no bad debts, then credit sales for the period would be as follows.

	£
Cash received from debtors	28,490
Plus closing debtors	3,140
Less opening debtors	(1,750)
Credit sales during the period	29,880

3.3 If there are bad debts during the period, the value of sales will be increased by the amount of bad debts written off, no matter whether they relate to opening debtors or credit sales during the current period.

3.4 The same calculation could be made in a T-account, with credit sales being the balancing figure to complete the account.

DEBTORS

	£		£
Opening balance b/f	1,750	Cash received	28,490
Credit sales (balancing figure)	29,880	Closing balance c/f	3,140
	31,630		31,630

3.5 The same interrelationship between credit sales, cash from debtors, and opening and closing debtors balances can be used to derive a missing figure for cash from debtors, or opening or closing debtors, given the values for the three other items. For example, if we know that opening debtors are £6,700, closing debtors are £3,200 and credit sales for the period are £69,400, then cash received from debtors during the period would be as follows.

DEBTORS

	£		£
Opening balance	6,700	Cash received (balancing figure)	72,900
Sales (on credit)	69,400	Closing balance c/f	3,200
	76,100		76,100

There is an alternative way of presenting the same calculation.

	£
Opening balance of debtors	6,700
Plus credit sales during the period	69,400
Total money owed to the business	76,100
Less closing balance of debtors	3,200
Equals cash received during the period	72,900

Control account

3.6 Control account reconciliations have been covered at the AAT Foundation stage, but some practice exercises are given in the *Financial Accounting* Workbook for revision as it is possible that you will be asked to reconcile control accounts in an incomplete records question or assessment. You should also remember the complications which might arise in a sales ledger control account, which might include the following.

SALES LEDGER CONTROL ACCOUNT

	£		£
Opening debit balances	X	Opening credit balances (if any)	X
Sales	X	Cash received	X
Dishonoured bills or cheques	X	Discounts allowed	X
Cash paid to clear credit balances	X	Returns inwards	X
Bad debts recovered	X	Bad debts	X
Closing credit balances	X	Cash from bad debts recovered	X
		Contra with P/L control a/c	X
		Allowances on goods damaged	X
		Closing debit balances	X
	X		X

3.7 If you have to find a balancing figure in the sales ledger control account, you may have to consider all the above items.

4 PURCHASES AND TRADE CREDITORS

4.1 A similar relationship to that discussed above exists between purchases of stock during a period, the opening and closing balances for trade creditors, and amounts paid to trade creditors during the period.

If we wish to calculate an unknown amount for purchases, the amount would be derived as follows.

	£
Payments to trade creditors during the period	X
Plus closing balance of trade creditors (since these represent purchases in the current period for which payment has not yet been made)	X
Less opening balance of trade creditors (these debts, paid in the current period, relate to purchases in a previous period)	(X)
Purchases during the period	X

4.2 For example, suppose that a business had trade creditors of £3,728 on 1 October 19X5 and trade creditors of £2,645 on 30 September 19X6. If payments to trade creditors during the year to 30 September 19X6 were £31,479, then purchases during the year can be derived as follows.

	£
Payments to trade creditors	31,479
Plus closing balance of trade creditors	2,645
Less opening balance of trade creditors	(3,728)
Purchases	30,396

4.3 The same calculation could be made in a T-account, with purchases being the balancing figure to complete the account.

CREDITORS

	£		£
Cash payments	31,479	Opening balance b/f	3,728
Closing balance c/f	2,645	Purchases (balancing figure)	30,396
	34,124		34,124

Control account

4.4 As already mentioned, the reconciliation of control accounts is revised briefly in the *Financial Accounting* Workbook. Once again, various complications can arise in the purchase ledger control account which you may have to consider.

PURCHASE LEDGER CONTROL ACCOUNT

	£		£
Opening debit balances (if any)	X	Opening credit balances	X
Cash paid	X	Purchases and other expenses	X
Discounts received	X	Cash received clearing debit	
Returns outwards	X	balances	X
Contras with S/L control a/c	X	Closing debit balances	X
Allowances on goods damaged	X		
Closing credit balances	X		
	X		X

5 PURCHASES, STOCKS AND COST OF SALES
Centrally assessed 6/94

5.1 When the value of purchases is not known, a different approach might be required to find out what they were, depending on the nature of the information given to you.

5.2 One approach would be to use information about the cost of sales, and opening and closing stocks. This means that you would be using the trading account rather than the trade creditors account to find the cost of purchases.

		£
Since:	opening stocks	X
	plus purchases	X
	less closing stocks	(X)
	equals the cost of goods sold	X

		£
then:	the cost of goods sold	X
	plus closing stocks	X
	less opening stocks	(X)
	equals purchases for the period	X

5.3 Suppose that the stock in trade of a business on 1 July 19X6 has a balance sheet value of £8,400, and a stock taking exercise at 30 June 19X7 showed stock to be valued at £9,350. Sales for the year to 30 June 19X7 are £80,000, and the business makes a mark up of $33^1/_3\%$ on cost for all the items that it sells. What were the purchases during the year?

5.4 The cost of goods sold can be derived from the value of sales, as follows.

		£
Sales	(133¹/₃%)	80,000
Gross profit	(33¹/₃%)	20,000
Cost of goods sold	(100%)	60,000

The cost of goods sold is 75% ($100\% \div 133^1/_3\%$) of sales value.

	£
Cost of goods sold	60,000
Plus closing stock	9,350
Less opening stock	(8,400)
Purchases during the period	60,950

5.5 A similar type of calculation might be required to derive the value of goods stolen or destroyed. An example will show how to determine the cost of an unknown quantity of goods lost.

Example: Stock lost in a fire

5.6 Orlean Flames is a shop which sells fashion clothes. On 1 January 19X5, it had stock in trade which cost £7,345. During the nine months to 30 September 19X5, the business purchased goods from suppliers costing £106,420. Sales during the same period were £154,000. The shop makes a mark-up of 40% on cost for everything it sells. On 30 September 19X5, there was a fire in the shop which destroyed most of the stock in it. Only a small amount of stock, known to have cost £350, was undamaged and still fit for sale.

How much stock was lost in the fire?

Solution: Stock lost in a fire

5.7

		£
(a)	Sales (140%)	154,000
	Gross profit (40%)	44,000
	Cost of goods sold (100%)	110,000

		£
(b)	Opening stock, at cost	7,345
	Plus purchases	106,420
		113,765
	Less closing stock, at cost	350
	Equals cost of goods sold and goods lost	113,415

		£
(c)	Cost of goods sold and lost	113,415
	Cost of goods sold	110,000
	Cost of goods lost	3,415

Example: Stock stolen

5.8 Beau Gullard runs a jewellery shop in the High Street. On 1 January 19X9, his stock in trade, at cost, amounted to £4,700 and his trade creditors were £3,950.

During the six months to 30 June 19X9, sales were £42,000. Beau Gullard makes a gross profit of 33¹/₃% on the sales value of everything he sells.

On 30 June, there was a burglary at the shop, and all the stock was stolen.

In trying to establish how much stock had been taken, Beau Gullard was able to provide the following information.

(a) He knew from his bank statements that he had paid £28,400 to creditors in the six month period to 30 June 19X9.

(b) He currently owed creditors £5,550.

Tasks

(a) Calculate how much stock was stolen.
(b) Prepare a trading account for the six months to 30 June 19X9.

Solution: Stock stolen

5.9 (a) We must establish some 'unknowns' before we can calculate how much stock was stolen.

(i) The first 'unknown' is the amount of purchases during the period. This is established by the method previously described in this chapter.

CREDITORS

	£		£
Payments to creditors	28,400	Opening balance b/f	3,950
Closing balance c/f	5,550	Purchases (balancing figure)	30,000
	33,950		33,950

(ii) The cost of goods sold is also unknown, but this can be established from the gross profit margin and the sales for the period.

		£
Sales	(100%)	42,000
Gross profit	(33¹/₃%)	14,000
Cost of goods sold	(66²/₃%)	28,000

(iii) The cost of the goods stolen is as follows.

	£
Opening stock at cost	4,700
Purchases	30,000
	34,700
Less closing stock (after burglary)	0
Cost of goods sold and goods stolen	34,700
Cost of goods sold (see (ii) above)	28,000
Cost of goods stolen	6,700

(b) The cost of the goods stolen will not be a charge in the trading account, and so the trading account for the period is as follows.

BEAU GULLARD
TRADING ACCOUNT FOR THE SIX MONTHS TO 30 JUNE 19X9

	£	£
Sales		42,000
Less cost of goods sold		
Opening stock	4,700	
Purchases	30,000	
	34,700	
Less stock stolen	6,700	
		28,000
Gross profit		14,000

5.10 You may have noticed that we have used two terms for the relationship between gross profit and either cost or sales.

(a) *Mark-up* is where the gross profit is calculated as a percentage of cost, for example the company makes a mark up of 30% on cost.

(b) *Gross profit margin* is usually used to denote the relationship between profit and sales, for example the company makes a gross profit of 25% on sales.

	Mark-up	*Gross profit percentage*
	%	%
Sales	130	100
Cost of sales	100	75
Mark up/gross profit margin	30	25

Accounting for stock lost

5.11 When stock is stolen, destroyed or otherwise lost, the loss must be accounted for somehow. Since the loss is an extraordinary one, the cost of the goods lost is not included in the trading account, as the previous example showed. The credit side of the accounting double entry is therefore made in the trading account. Instead of showing the cost of the loss as a credit, it is usually shown as a deduction on the debit side of the trading account, which is the same as a 'plus' on the credit side.

5.12 There are two possible accounts that could be debited with the other side of the accounting double entry, depending on whether or not the lost goods were insured.

(a) If the lost goods were not insured the business must bear the loss and the loss is shown in the P & L account.

DEBIT   Profit and loss
CREDIT   Trading account

(b) If the lost goods were insured the business will not suffer a loss because the insurance will pay back the cost of the lost goods. This means that there is no charge at all in the P & L account, and the appropriate double entry for the cost of the loss is as follows.

DEBIT   Insurance claim account (debtor account)
CREDIT   Trading account

The insurance claim will then be a current asset, and shown in the balance sheet of the business as such. When the claim is paid, the account is then closed.

DEBIT   Cash
CREDIT   Insurance claim account

6   THE CASH BOOK
Centrally assessed 12/94

6.1 The construction of a cash book, largely from bank statements showing receipts and payments of a business during a given period, is often an important feature of incomplete records problems. The purpose of an incomplete records exercise is largely to test your understanding about how various items of receipts or payments relate to the preparation of a final set of accounts for a business.

6.2   We have already seen in this chapter that information about cash receipts or payments might be needed to establish the amount of credit sales or of purchases during a period.

Other items of receipts or payments might be relevant to establishing:

(a)   the amount of cash sales;
(b)   the amount of certain expenses in the profit and loss account;
(c)   the amount of drawings by the business proprietor.

6.3   It might therefore be helpful, if a business does not keep a cash book on a daily basis, to construct a cash book at the end of an accounting period. A business which typically might not keep a daily cash book is a shop.

(a)   Many sales, if not all sales, are cash sales and payment is received in the form of notes and coins, cheques, or credit cards at the time of sale.

(b)   Some payments are made in notes and coins out of the till rather than by payment out of the business bank account by cheque.

6.4   Where there appears to be a sizeable volume of receipts and payments in cash then it is also helpful to construct a *two column cash book*. This is a cash book with one column for receipts and payments, and one column for money paid into and out of the business bank account.

Example: Preparing a cash book

6.5   Jonathan Slugg owns and runs a shop selling fishing tackle, making a gross profit of 25% on the cost of everything he sells. He does not keep a cash book.

On 1 January 19X7 the balance sheet of his business was as follows.

	£	£
Net fixed assets		20,000
Stock	10,000	
Cash in the bank	3,000	
Cash in the till	200	
	13,200	
Trade creditors	1,200	
		12,000
		32,000
Proprietor's capital		32,000

You are given the following information about the year to 31 December 19X7.

(a)   There were no sales on credit.

(b)   £41,750 in receipts were banked.

(c)   The bank statements of the period show the payments:

(i)	to trade creditors	£36,000
(ii)	sundry expenses	£5,600
(iii)	in drawings	£4,400

(d)   Payments were also made in cash out of the till:

(i)	to trade creditors	£800
(ii)	sundry expenses	£1,500
(iii)	in drawings	£3,700

At 31 December 19X7, the business had cash in the till of £450 and trade creditors of £1,400. The cash balance in the bank was not known and the value of closing stock has not yet been calculated. There were no accruals or prepayments. No further fixed assets were purchased during the year. The depreciation charge for the year is £900.

Tasks

(a) Prepare a two-column cash book for the period.

(b) Prepare the trading, profit and loss account for the year to 31 December 19X7 and the balance sheet as at 31 December 19X7.

Discussion and solution: Preparing a cash book

6.6 A two-column cash book is completed as follows.

(a) Enter the opening cash balances.

(b) Enter the information given about cash payments (and any cash receipts, if there had been any such items given in the problem).

(c) The cash receipts banked are a 'contra' entry, being both a debit (bank column) and a credit (cash in hand column) in the same account.

(d) Enter the closing cash in hand (cash in the bank at the end of the period is not known).

CASH BOOK

	Cash in hand £	Bank £		Cash in hand £	Bank £
Balance b/f	200	3,000	Trade creditors	800	36,000
Cash receipts			Sundry expenses	1,500	5,600
banked (contra)		41,750	Drawings	3,700	4,400
Sales	*48,000		Cash receipts banked		
Balance c/f		*1,250	(contra)	41,750	
			Balance c/f	450	
	48,200	46,000		48,200	46,000

★ Balancing figures

(e) The closing balance of money in the bank is a balancing figure.

(f) Since all sales are for cash, a balancing figure that can be entered in the cash book is sales, in the cash in hand (debit) column.

6.7 It is important to notice that since not all receipts from cash sales are banked, the value of cash sales during the period is as follows.

	£
Receipts banked	41,750
Plus expenses and drawings paid out of the till in cash	
£(800 + 1,500 + 3,700)	6,000
Plus any cash stolen (here there is none)	0
Plus the closing balance of cash in hand	450
	48,200
Less the opening balance of cash in hand	(200)
Equals cash sales	48,000

6.8 The cash book constructed in this way has enabled us to establish both the closing balance for cash in the bank and also the volume of cash sales. The trading, profit and loss account and the balance sheet can also be prepared, once a value for purchases has been calculated.

CREDITORS

	£		£
Cash book:		Balance b/f	1,200
payments from bank	36,000	Purchases (balancing figure)	37,000
Cash book:			
payments in cash	800		
Balance c/f	1,400		
	38,200		38,200

The mark-up of 25% on cost indicates that the cost of the goods sold is £38,400, as follows.

	£
Sales (125%)	48,000
Gross profit (25%)	9,600
Cost of goods sold (100%)	38,400

The closing stock amount is now a balancing figure in the trading account.

JONATHAN SLUGG TRADING, PROFIT AND LOSS ACCOUNT
FOR THE YEAR ENDED 31 DECEMBER 19X7

	£	£
Sales		48,000
Less cost of goods sold		
Opening stock	10,000	
Purchases	37,000	
	47,000	
Less closing stock (balancing figure)	8,600	
		38,400
Gross profit (25/125 × £48,000)		9,600
Expenses		
Sundry £(1,500 + 5,600)	7,100	
Depreciation	900	
		8,000
Net profit		1,600

JONATHAN SLUGG
BALANCE SHEET AS AT 31 DECEMBER 19X7

	£	£
Net fixed assets £(20,000 – 900)		19,100
Stock	8,600	
Cash in the till	450	
	9,050	
Bank overdraft	1,250	
Trade creditors	1,400	
	2,650	
Net current assets		6,400
		25,500
Proprietor's capital		
Balance b/f		32,000
Net profit for the year		1,600
		33,600
Drawings £(3,700 + 4,400)		(8,100)
Balance c/f		25,500

Theft of cash from the till

6.9 When cash is stolen from the till, the amount stolen will be a credit entry in the cash book, and a debit in either the profit and loss account or insurance claim account, depending on whether the business is insured. The missing figure for cash sales, if this has to be calculated, must take account of cash received but later stolen: see Paragraph 6.7.

Using a debtors account to calculate both cash sales and credit sales

6.10 Another point which needs to be considered is how a missing value can be found for cash sales and credit sales, when a business has both, but takings banked by the business are not divided between takings from cash sales and takings from credit sales.

Example: Determining the value of sales during the period

6.11   Suppose, for example, that a business had, on 1 January 19X8, trade debtors of £2,000, cash in the bank of £3,000, and cash in hand of £300.

During the year to 31 December 19X8 the business banked £95,000 in takings. It also paid out the following expenses in cash from the till.

Drawings	£1,200
Sundry expenses	£800

On 29 August 19X8 a thief broke into the shop and stole £400 from the till.

At 31 December 19X8 trade debtors amounted to £3,500, cash in the bank £2,500 and cash in the till £150.

What was the value of sales during the year?

Solution: Determining the value of sales during the period

6.12   If we tried to prepare a debtors account and a two column cash book, we would have insufficient information, in particular about whether the takings which were banked related to cash sales or credit sales.

DEBTORS

	£		£
Balance b/f	2,000	Payments from debtors	
Credit sales	*Unknown*	(credit sales)	*Unknown*
		Balance c/f	3,500

CASH BOOK

	Cash £	Bank £		Cash £	Bank £
Balance b/f	300	3,000	Drawings	1,200	
			Sundry expenses	800	
Debtors: payments		*Unknown*	Cash stolen	400	
Cash sales		*Unknown*	Balance c/f	150	2,500

All we do know is that the combined sums from debtors and cash takings banked is £95,000.

The value of sales can be found instead by using the debtors account, which should be used to record cash takings banked as well as payments by debtors. The balancing figure in the debtors account will then be a combination of credit sales and some cash sales. The cash book only needs to have single columns.

DEBTORS

	£		£
Balance b/f	2,000	Cash banked	95,000
Sales to trading account	96,500	Balance c/f	3,500
	98,500		98,500

CASH (EXTRACT)

	£		£
Balance in hand b/f	300	*Payments in cash*	
Balance in bank b/f	3,000	Drawings	1,200
Debtors a/c	95,000	Expenses	800
		Other payments	?
		Cash stolen	400
		Balance in hand c/f	150
		Balance in bank c/f	2,500

The remaining 'undiscovered' amount of cash sales is now found as follows.

	£
Payments in cash out of the till	
Drawings	1,200
Expenses	800
	2,000
Cash stolen	400
Closing balance of cash in hand	150
	2,550
Less opening balance of cash in hand	(300)
Further cash sales	2,250

(This calculation is similar to the one described in Paragraph 6.7.)

Total sales for the year	£
From debtors account	96,500
From cash book	2,250
Total sales	98,750

7 ACCRUALS AND PREPAYMENTS

7.1 Where there is an accrued expense or a prepayment, the charge to be made in the P&L account for the item concerned should be found from the opening balance b/f, the closing balance c/f, and cash payments for the item during the period. The charge in the P & L account is perhaps most easily found as the balancing figure in a T-account.

7.2 For example, suppose that on 1 April 19X6 a business had prepaid rent of £700 which relates to the next accounting period. During the year to 31 March 19X7 it pays £9,300 in rent, and at 31 March 19X7 the prepayment of rent is £1,000. The cost of rent in the P & L account for the year to 31 March 19X7 would be the balancing figure in the following T-account. (Remember that a prepayment is a current asset, and so is a debit balance brought forward.)

RENT

	£		£
Prepayment: balance b/f	700	P & L account (balancing figure)	9,000
Cash	9,300	Prepayment: balance c/f	1,000
	10,000		10,000
Balance b/f	1,000		

7.3 Similarly, if a business has accrued telephone expenses as at 1 July 19X6 of £850, pays £6,720 in telephone bills during the year to 30 June 19X7, and has accrued telephone expenses of £1,140 as at 30 June 19X7, then the telephone expense to be shown in the P&L account for the year to 30 June 19X7 is the balancing figure in the following T-account. (Remember that an accrual is a current liability, and so is a credit balance brought forward.)

TELEPHONE EXPENSES

	£		£
Cash	6,720	Balance b/f (accrual)	850
Balance c/f (accrual)	1,140	P & L a/c (balancing figure)	7,010
	7,860		7,860
		Balance b/f	1,140

8 DRAWINGS
Centrally assessed 6/94, 12/94, 6/95

8.1 In the case of a sole trader, drawings would normally represent no particular problem at all in preparing a set of final accounts from incomplete records, but it is not unusual for questions to involve the following situations.

(a) The business owner pays income into his bank account which has nothing whatever to do with the business operations. For example, the owner might pay dividend income or other income from investments into the bank, from stocks and shares which he owns personally, separate from the business itself.

(b) The business owner pays money out of the business bank account for items which are not business expenses, such as life insurance premiums or a payment for his family's holidays.

(c) The owner takes stock for his personal use.

8.2   These personal items of receipts or payments should be dealt with as follows.

(a) *Receipts* should be set off against drawings. For example, if a business owner receives £600 in dividend income from investments not owned by the business and pays it into the business bank account, then the accounting entry is as follows.

DEBIT   Cash
CREDIT   Drawings

(b) *Payments of cash for personal items* should be charged to drawings.

DEBIT   Drawings
CREDIT   Cash

(c) *Goods taken for personal use* (drawings of stock): the traditional way of dealing with this has been to charge the goods to drawings at cost. The required entries are:

DEBIT   Drawings
CREDIT   Purchases

However, the AAT's recommended treatment, according better with modern practice and the requirements of HM Customs & Excise, is as follows.

DEBIT   Drawings at selling price (including VAT)
CREDIT   Sales
CREDIT   VAT

In the March 1995 edition of the *Education and Training Newsletter*, acknowledging the variation in practice and between different VAT offices, the AAT stated that the traditional method would be accepted, but you should try to use the newer, recommended method if information on VAT is available.

This is regularly tested in central assessment tasks, so be warned!

8.3   You should also note the following warnings.

(a) If an exercise states that a proprietor's drawings during a given year are 'approximately £40 per week' then you should assume that drawings for the year are £40 × 52 weeks = £2,080.

(b) However, if an exercise states that drawings in the year are 'between £35 and £45 per week', do not assume that the drawings average £40 per week and so amount to £2,080 for the year. You could not be certain that the actual drawings did average £40, and so you should treat the drawings figure as a missing item that needs to be calculated.

9   USING SIMPLE ACCOUNTING RATIOS

9.1   An incomplete records exercise may require you to use simple accounting ratios to derive missing information. We have already seen how to use the profit margin and profit mark-up percentages to identify missing values but there are a few more ratios that you should know about.

9.2 The formulae for calculating the ratios may vary and you should check the wording of the question to determine the basis of calculation. The ratios which you are most likely to meet are as follows.

(a) *Current ratio* $= \dfrac{\text{Current assets}}{\text{Current liabilities}}$

This ratio is used to assess whether a business is sufficiently liquid, ie whether its current assets are sufficient to cover its current liabilities.

(b) *Quick ratio* $= \dfrac{\text{Current assets} - \text{Stock}}{\text{Current liabilities}}$

This ratio goes one step further than the current ratio in assessing liquidity. It 'removes' the less liquid asset of stock from the calculation to see whether the remaining current assets are sufficient to cover the current liabilities.

(c) *Debtors payment period* $= \dfrac{\text{Debtors}}{\text{Sales}} \times 365 \text{ days}$

This ratio measures the number of days debt which is outstanding, so that managers can monitor the level of credit being given to customers.

(d) *Creditors payment period* $= \dfrac{\text{Creditors}}{\text{Purchases}} \times 365 \text{ days}$

This ratio monitors the number of days credit which is being taken from suppliers.

(e) *Number of days stock* $= \dfrac{\text{Stock (average or year end)}}{\text{Cost of sales}} \times 365 \text{ days}$

This ratio converts the stock figure into the number of days cost of sales, to monitor the level of stock in the business.

(f) *Stock turnover* $= \dfrac{\text{Cost of sales}}{\text{Average stock}}$ or $\dfrac{\text{Cost of sales}}{\text{Year end stock}}$

This ratio is similar to (e) in that it monitors the level of stockholding. The higher the stock turnover, the less time on average each stock item is held.

9.3 An example will illustrate how these ratios can be used to derive missing information.

Example: Using accounting ratios

9.4 Toasty Heating purchases central heating boilers and sells them at a gross profit margin of 40% of sales price. All sales and purchases are made on credit.

Information relating to 19X6 is as follows.

	£
Sales during the year	620,500
Purchases during the year	365,000
Accrued expenses as at 31 December 19X6	3,000
Prepaid expenses as at 31 December 19X6	4,000
Net book value of fixed assets as at 31 December 19X6	38,000

The number of days stock held by the business (year end stock divided by cost of sales multiplied by 365 days) is 29 days.

The debtors payment period (year end debtors divided by sales multiplied by 365 days) is 27 days and the creditors payment period (year end creditors divided by purchases multiplied by 365 days) is 37 days.

The ratio of current assets to current liabilities on 31 December 19X6 was 2.1:1.

Task

Prepare the balance sheet for Toasty Heating as at 31 December 19X6.

Solution: Using accounting ratios

9.5 *Workings*

(1) Cost of sales

$$= 60\% \times \text{sales value}$$
$$= 60\% \times £620,500$$
$$= £372,300$$

(2) Number of days stock

$$= \frac{\text{Year end stock}}{\text{Cost of sales}} \times 365$$

$$\therefore 29 = \frac{\text{Year end stock}}{£372,300} \times 365$$

$$\text{Year end stock} = £372,300 \times 29/365 = £29,580$$

(3) Debtors payment period

$$= \frac{\text{Year end debtors}}{\text{Sales}} \times 365$$

$$\therefore 27 = \frac{\text{Year end debtors}}{£620,500} \times 365$$

$$\text{Year end debtors} = £620,500 \times 27/365 = £45,900$$

(4) Creditors payment period

$$= \frac{\text{Year end creditors}}{\text{Purchases}} \times 365$$

$$\therefore 37 = \frac{\text{Year end creditors}}{£365,000} \times 365$$

$$\text{Year end creditors} = £365,000 \times 37/365 = £37,000$$

(5) Total current liabilities

$$= \text{Creditors} + \text{Accrued expenses}$$
$$= £37,000 + £3,000 = £40,000$$

Current assets: current liabilities = 2.1:1

∴ current assets = $2.1 \times £40,000 = £84,000$

TOASTY HEATING
BALANCE SHEET AS AT 31 DECEMBER 19X6

	£	£
Fixed assets		38,000
Current assets		
Stock (W2)	29,580	
Debtors (W3)	45,900	
Prepaid expenses	4,000	
Bank/cash (balancing figure)	4,520	
Total current assets (W5)	84,000	
Current liabilities		
Creditors (W4)	37,000	
Accrued expenses	3,000	
	40,000	
Net current assets		44,000
		82,000
Proprietor's capital as at 31 December 19X6		82,000

10 COMPREHENSIVE EXAMPLE

10.1 A suggested approach to dealing with incomplete records problems brings together the various points described so far in this chapter. The nature of the 'incompleteness' in the records will vary from problem to problem, but the approach, suitably applied, should be successful in arriving at the final accounts whatever the particular characteristics of the problem might be.

10.2   The approach is as follows.

Step 1. If it is not already known, establish the opening balance sheet and the brought forward profit and loss account balance if possible.

Step 2. Open up four accounts.

(1)   A trading account (if you wish, leave space underneath for entering the P & L account later)

(2)   A cash book, with two columns if cash sales are significant and there are payments in cash out of the till

(3)   A debtors account

(4)   A creditors account

Step 3. Enter the opening balances in these accounts.

Step 4. Work through the information you are given line by line. Each item should be entered into the appropriate account if it is relevant to one or more of these four accounts.

You should also try to recognise each item as a 'P & L account income or expense item' or a 'closing balance sheet item'.

It may be necessary to calculate an amount for drawings and an amount for fixed asset depreciation.

Step 5. Look for the balancing figures in your accounts. In particular you might be looking for a value for credit sales, cash sales, purchases, the cost of goods sold, the cost of goods stolen or destroyed, or the closing bank balance. Calculate these missing figures and make any necessary double entry (for example to the trading account from the creditors account for purchases, to the trading account from the cash book for cash sales, and to the trading account from the debtors account for credit sales).

Step 6. Now complete the P & L account and balance sheet. Working T-accounts might be needed where there are accruals or prepayments.

Example: Incomplete records

10.3   Whitton Ltd is the sole distribution agent in the Hillyard area for Squareup floor tiles. Under an agreement with the manufacturers, Whitton Ltd purchases the Squareup floor tiles at a trade discount of 20% off list price and annually in May receives an agency commission of 1% of the company's purchases for the year ended on the previous 31 March.

For several years, Whitton Ltd has obtained a gross profit of 40% on all sales. In a burglary in January 19X1 Whitton Ltd lost stock costing £4,000 as well as many accounting records. However, after careful investigations, the following information has been obtained covering the year ended 31 March 19X1.

(a)   Assets and liabilities at 31 March 19X0 were as follows.

	£
Buildings: at cost	10,000
provision for depreciation	6,000
Motor vehicles: at cost	5,000
provision for depreciation	2,000
Stock: at cost	3,200
Trade debtors (for sales)	6,300
Agency commission due	300
Prepayments (trade expenses)	120
Balance at bank	4,310
Trade creditors	4,200
Accrued vehicle expenses	230
Share capital	2,000

(b)   Whitton Ltd has been notified that it will receive an agency commission of £440 on 1 May 19X1.

(c) Stock, at cost, at 31 March 19X1 was valued at an amount £3,000 more than a year previously.

(d) In October 19X0 stock costing £1,000 was damaged by damp and had to be scrapped as worthless.

(e) Trade creditors at 31 March 19X1 related entirely to goods received whose list prices totalled £9,500.

(f) Discounts allowed amounted to £1,620 whilst discounts received were £1,200.

(g) Trade expenses prepaid at 31 March 19X1 totalled £80.

(h) Vehicle expenses for the year ended 31 March 19X1 amounted to £7,020.

(i) Trade debtors (for sales) at 31 March 19X1 were £6,700.

(j) All receipts are passed through the bank account.

(k) Depreciation is provided annually at the rate of 5% on cost for buildings and 20% on cost for motor vehicles.

(l) Commissions received are paid directly to the bank account.

(m) In addition to the payments for purchases, the bank payments were as follows.

	£
Vehicle expenses	6,720
Wages	4,300
Trade expenses	7,360

(n) Whitton Ltd is not insured against loss of stock owing to burglary or damage to stock caused by damp.

Task

Prepare Whitton Ltd's trading and profit and loss account for the year ended 31 March 19X1 and a balance sheet on that date.

Discussion and solution: Incomplete records

10.4 This is an incomplete records problem because we are told that Whitton Ltd has lost many of its accounting records. In particular we do not know sales for the year, purchases during the year, or all the cash receipts and payments.

10.5 The first step is to find the opening balance sheet, if possible. In this case, it is. The profit and loss account balance is the balancing figure.

WHITTON LIMITED
BALANCE SHEET AS AT 31 MARCH 19X0

	Cost	Dep'n	
	£	£	£
Fixed assets			
Buildings	10,000	6,000	4,000
Motor vehicles	5,000	2,000	3,000
	15,000	8,000	7,000
Current assets			
Stock		3,200	
Trade debtors		6,300	
Commission due		300	
Prepayments		120	
Balance at bank		4,310	
		14,230	
Current liabilities			
Trade creditors		4,200	
Accrued expenses		230	
		4,430	
Net current assets			9,800
			16,800

	£
Capital and reserves	
Share capital	2,000
Profit and loss account (balance)	14,800
	16,800

10.6 The next step is to open up a trading account, cash book, debtors account and creditors account and to insert the opening balances, if known. Cash sales and payments in cash are not a feature of the problem, and so a single column cash book is sufficient.

10.7 The problem should then be read line by line, identifying any transactions affecting those accounts. (Notes refer to notes 1 - 9 given after the balance sheet below.)

TRADING ACCOUNT

	£	£
Sales (note (7))		60,000
Less cost of goods sold		
Opening stock	3,200	
Purchases (note (1))	44,000	
	47,200	
Less: damaged stock written off (note (3))	(1,000)	
stock stolen (note (6))	(4,000)	
	42,200	
Less closing stock (note (2))	6,200	
		36,000
Gross profit (note (7))		24,000

CASH BOOK

	£		£
Opening balance	4,310	Trade creditors	
Trade debtors (see below)	57,980	(see creditors a/c)	37,500
Agency commission (note (1))	300	Trade expenses	7,360
		Vehicle expenses	6,720
		Wages	4,300
		Balance c/f	6,710
	62,590		62,590

TRADE DEBTORS

	£		£
Opening balance b/f	6,300	Discounts allowed (note (4))	1,620
Sales (note (7))	60,000	Cash received (balancing figure)	57,980
		Closing balance c/f	6,700
	66,300		66,300

TRADE CREDITORS

	£		£
Discounts received (note (4))	1,200	Opening balance b/f	4,200
Cash paid (balancing figure)	37,500	Purchases (note (1))	44,000
Closing balance c/f (note (5))	9,500		
	48,200		48,200

VEHICLE EXPENSES

	£		£
Cash	6,720	Accrual b/f	230
Accrual c/f (balancing figure)	530	P & L account	7,020
	7,250		7,250

10.8 The trading account is complete already, but now the profit and loss account and balance sheet can be prepared. Do not forget items such as the stock losses, commission earned on purchases, discounts allowed and discounts received.

WHITTON LIMITED
TRADING, PROFIT AND LOSS ACCOUNT
FOR THE YEAR ENDED 31 MARCH 19X1

	£	£
Sales (note (7))		60,000
Less cost of goods sold		
Opening stock	3,200	
Purchases (note (1))	44,000	
	47,200	
Less: damaged stock written off (note (3))	(1,000)	
stock stolen (note (6))	(4,000)	
	42,200	
Less closing stock (note (2))	6,200	
		36,000
Gross profit (note (7))		24,000
Add: commission on purchases		440
discounts received (notes (4) and (5))		1,200
		25,640
Expenses		
Trade expenses (note (9))	7,400	
Wages	4,300	
Stock damaged	1,000	
Stock stolen	4,000	
Vehicle expenses	7,020	
Discounts allowed (notes (4) and (5))	1,620	
Depreciation		
Buildings (5% × £10,000)	500	
Motor vehicles (20% × £5,000)	1,000	
		26,840
Loss for the year		(1,200)

WHITTON LIMITED
BALANCE SHEET AS AT 31 MARCH 19X1

	Cost £	Dep'n £	NBV £
Fixed assets			
Buildings	10,000	6,500	3,500
Motor vehicles	5,000	3,000	2,000
	15,000	9,500	5,500
Current assets			
Stock		6,200	
Trade debtors		6,700	
Commission due		440	
Prepayments (trade expenses)		80	
Balance at bank		6,710	
		20,130	
Current liabilities			
Trade creditors		9,500	
Accrued expenses		530	
		10,030	
			10,100
			15,600
Capital and reserves			
Share capital			2,000
Profit and loss account (£14,800 – £1,200)			13,600
			15,600

Notes

(1) The agency commission due on 1 May 19X1 indicates that purchases for the year to 31 March 19X1 were 100%/1% × £440 = £44,000.

(2) Closing stock at cost on 31 March 19X1 was £(3,200 + 3,000) = £6,200.

(3) Stock scrapped (£1,000) is accounted for as follows.

CREDIT   Trading account
DEBIT   P&L account

(4) Discounts allowed and discounts received are accounted for as follows.

DEBIT   Discounts allowed account
CREDIT   Debtors

DEBIT   Creditors
CREDIT   Discounts received

(5) Discounts on outstanding creditor balances should not be anticipated (unless perhaps the discounts are agreed under written contracts) because this anticipates profit (ie creditors are decreased and profit is increased), against the prudence concept. If you did take account of the discounts receivable and outstanding creditor balances, then the following figures would be different.

Creditors closing balance c/f = £9,500 – (20% × £9,500) = £7,600
Discounts received = £1,200 + (£9,500 × 20%) = £3,100

The loss for the year is therefore turned into a profit of £1,200 + (£9,500 × 20%) = £700, which makes the accounts look a lot better!

(6) Stocks lost in the burglary are accounted for by the following accounting entries.

CREDIT   Trading account
DEBIT   P&L account

(7) The trade discount of 20% is deducted in arriving at the value of the purchases. The gross profit is 40% on sales, so with cost of sales of £36,000 the sales value can be calculated as £60,000.

		£
Cost	(60%)	36,000
Profit	(40%)	24,000
Sales	(100%)	60,000

It is assumed that trade expenses are not included in the trading account, and so should be ignored in this calculation.

(8) The agency commission of £300 due on 1 May 19X0 would have been paid to John Snow at that date.

(9) The P & L account expenditure for trade expenses and closing balance on vehicle expenses account are as follows.

TRADE EXPENSES

	£		£
Prepayment	120	P&L account (balancing figure)	7,400
Cash	7,360	Prepayment c/f	80
	7,480		7,480

Key points in this chapter

- If the relevant information is available, an *opening balance sheet* should be prepared.

- *Debtor* and *creditor* accounts can be used to find balancing figures, namely:

  o opening debtors and creditors;
  o closing debtors and creditors;
  o cash paid/cash received.

- The *cash book* should be divided into cash and bank balances.

- *Accounting ratios* can be used to find either sales or cost of sales figures.

For practice on the points covered in this chapter you should now attempt the Practice Exercises in Session 8 of the Financial Accounting Workbook

9 Club accounts and manufacturing accounts

This chapter covers the following topics.

1 The accounts of a non-trading organisation

2 The receipts and payments account

3 Preparing income and expenditure accounts

4 Manufacturing accounts

1 THE ACCOUNTS OF A NON-TRADING ORGANISATION

1.1 So far you have dealt with the accounts of businesses. In the first three sections of this chapter we consider *non-trading organisations*, that is organisations which are not incorporated under the Companies Act and whose objectives are to provide services to their members or the pursuit of one or a number of activities rather than the earning of profit.

1.2 Such entities may be, and often are, very small in both membership and wealth. However, they can also be very large like the Automobile Association, which in 1994 had nearly 8 million members and net assets with a book value of over £400 million.

1.3 So long as subscriptions are charged, there will be a need for some financial records, the minimum possible being a cash book and petty cash book. Clubs which rely on this minimum package often confine their annual accounts to a *receipts and payments account*. This is simply a summary of cash received and paid for a period, and is discussed in Section 2 of this chapter.

1.4 A receipts and payments account may be adequate for some clubs, but it has important deficiencies when used by clubs which have substantial assets (in addition to cash) and liabilities. The arguments in favour of accruals based accounting apply to clubs as well as profit making entities, and most large clubs do produce financial statements based on accruals accounting. In particular many clubs produce what is basically a profit and loss account but they call it an *income and expenditure account*. This is the subject of Section 3 of this chapter.

1.5 Since a non-trading organisation does not exist to make a profit, it is wrong to refer to its 'profit and loss' account. However, a non-trading organisation must be able to pay its way, and so it is still important to ensure that income covers expenses. For this reason, an 'income and expenditure' account, together with a balance sheet, is an important report for judging the financial affairs of the organisation. The principles of 'accruals' accounting (the matching concept) are applied to income and expenditure accounts in the same way as for profit and loss accounts.

1.6 An income and expenditure account is simply the name that is given to what is effectively the profit and loss account of a non-trading organisation, such as sports clubs, social clubs, societies and other associations, charities and so on.

1.7 There are one or two differences between the final accounts of a non-trading organisation and those of a business.

(a) Since non-trading organisations do not exist to make profits, the difference between income and matching expenditure in the *income and expenditure account* is referred to as a *surplus* or a *deficit* rather than a profit or loss.

(b) The capital or proprietorship of the organisation is referred to as the *accumulated fund*, rather than the capital account. In addition, other separate funds might be kept by the organisation (see Paragraph 1.11).

(c) There is usually no separate trading account. Instead, it is usual to net off expenditure against income for like items. To explain this point further, it will be useful to consider the sources of income for a non-trading organisation in further detail.

Sources of income for non-trading organisations

1.8 Non-trading organisations differ in purpose and character, but we shall concentrate here on sports clubs, social clubs or societies. These will obtain their income from various sources which include the following.

(a) Membership subscriptions for annual membership of the club (and initial joining subscriptions for first year members)

(b) Payments for life membership

(c) 'Profits' from bar sales

(d) 'Profits' from the sale of food in the club restaurant or cafeteria

(e) 'Profits' from social events, such as dinner-dances

(f) Interest received on investments

1.9 *Netting off* expenditure against income for like items means that where some sources of income have associated costs, the net surplus or deficit should be shown in the income and expenditure account.

(a) If a club holds an annual dinner-dance, for example, the income and expenditure account will net off the costs of the event against the revenue to show the surplus or deficit.

(b) Similarly, if a club has a bar, the income and expenditure account will show the surplus or deficit on its trading. Although the organisation itself does not trade, the bar within the organisation does, and so it is in fact correct to refer to 'profits' from the bar.

1.10 Where there is trading activity within a non-trading organisation (eg bar sales, cafeteria sales etc) so that the organisation must hold stocks of drink or food etc it is usual to prepare a trading account for that particular activity, and then to record the surplus or deficit from trading in the income and expenditure account. An example is shown below.

FOOLSMATE CHESS CLUB
BAR TRADING ACCOUNT FOR THE YEAR TO 31 DECEMBER 19X5

	£	£
Sales		18,000
Less cost of goods sold		
Bar stocks 1 January 19X5	1,200	
Purchases	15,400	
	16,600	
Less bar stocks at 31 December 19X5	1,600	
		15,000
Bar profit (taken to income and expenditure account)		3,000

Funds of non-trading organisations

1.11 Although the capital of a non-trading organisation is generally accounted for as the accumulated fund, some *separate funds* might be set up for particular purposes.

(a) A *life membership fund* is a fund for the money subscribed for life membership by various members of the organisation. The money paid for life membership is commonly invested outside the organisation (for example in a building society account). The investment then earns interest for the organisation.

(b) A *building fund* might be set up whereby the organisation sets aside money to save for the cost of a new building extension. The money put into the fund will be invested outside the organisation, earning interest, until it is eventually needed for the building work. It might take several years to create a fund large enough for the building work planned.

1.12 The basic principles of accounting for special funds are as follows.

(a) When money is put into the fund:
DEBIT   Cash
CREDIT   Special-purpose fund

(b) When the cash is invested:

DEBIT   Investments (eg building society account)
CREDIT   Cash

(c) When the investments earn interest:

DEBIT   Cash
CREDIT   Interest received account (and subsequently, the income and expenditure account, or possibly the fund account itself).

2   THE RECEIPTS AND PAYMENTS ACCOUNT

2.1   Many small charities and clubs have little, if any, accounting expertise and keep records only of cash paid and received. The receipts and payments account is effectively a summary of an organisation's cash book. To facilitate the production of such a financial statement an *analysed cash book* will probably be used. No balance sheet is produced with a receipts and payments account.

Example: Receipts and payments account

2.2

HIGH LEE STRONG TENNIS CLUB
RECEIPTS AND PAYMENTS ACCOUNT
FOR THE YEAR ENDED 30 APRIL 19X0

Receipts	£	Payments	£
Balance b/f	16	Bar expenses	106
Bar takings	160	Rent	50
Subscriptions	328	Wages	140
		Postage	10
		Printing	12
		Affiliation fees to LTS	18
		Lawn mower*	50
		Heat and light	60
		Balance c/f	58
	504		504

*Item of capital expenditure

2.3   The *advantages* of this type of financial statement are as follows.

(a) It is very easy to produce and understand.

(b) It serves as a basis for the preparation of the income and expenditure account and balance sheet.

2.4   In isolation, the receipts and payments account has some *disadvantages*.

(a) It takes no account of any amounts owing or prepaid.

(b) It includes items of capital expenditure and makes no distinction between capital and revenue items.

(c) It takes no account of depreciation of fixed assets.

2.5   For the layman, however, particularly in the case of small clubs where the transactions are simple and straightforward, a receipts and payments account will be sufficient.

3   PREPARING INCOME AND EXPENDITURE ACCOUNTS

3.1   You may in practice be provided with a receipts and payments account, balances of assets and liabilities at the beginning of the period, and details of accruals and prepayments at the end of the period. You would be required typically to perform the following tasks.

(a) Calculate the balance on the accumulated fund at the beginning of the period.
(b) Prepare a trading account for a particular activity for the period.
(c) Prepare an income and expenditure account for the period.
(d) Prepare a balance sheet at the end of the period.

3.2 Before looking at an example of an income and expenditure account we need to look at each of the following items in some detail.

(a) Membership subscriptions
(b) Bar trading account
(c) Life membership

These are items which we have not yet come across in previous chapters of this Tutorial Text, because they are not found in the accounts of businesses. We must not forget, however, that in many respects the accounts of non-trading organisations are similar to those of businesses with fixed assets, a provision for depreciation, current assets and current liabilities, expense accounts (eg electricity, telephone, stationery etc) accruals and prepayments.

Membership subscriptions

3.3 Annual membership subscriptions of clubs and societies are usually payable one year in advance.

A club or society therefore receives payments from members for benefits which the members have yet to enjoy, and so payments in advance by members, being receipts in advance to the club or society, will be shown in the balance sheet of the society as a current liability, to the extent that the year's membership has still to run as at the balance sheet date.

3.4 A numerical example might help to clarify this point.

The Mudflannels Cricket Club charges an annual membership of £50 payable in advance on 1 October each year. All 40 members pay their subscriptions promptly on 1 October 19X4. If the club's accounting year ends on 31 December total subscriptions of 40 × £50 = £2,000 would be treated as follows.

(a) $40 \times \dfrac{9 \text{ months}}{12 \text{ months}} \times £50 = £1,500$ will appear in the balance sheet of the club as at

31 December 19X4 as a current liability 'subscriptions in advance'. These subscriptions relate to the period 1 January to 30 September 19X5.

(b) $40 \times \dfrac{3 \text{ months}}{12 \text{ months}} \times £50 = £500$ will appear as income in the income and

expenditure account for the period 1 October to 31 December 19X4.

3.5 When members are in arrears with subscriptions and owe money to the club or society, they are 'debtors' of the organisation and so appear as current assets in the balance sheet under 'subscriptions in arrears'. These should be shown as a separate item in the balance sheet, and should not be netted off against subscriptions in advance.

3.6 For example, suppose that the Bluespot Squash Club has 100 members, each of whom pays an annual membership of £60 on 1 November. Of those 100 members, 90 pay their subscriptions before 31 December 19X5 (for the 19X5/X6 year) but 10 have still not paid. If the club's accounting year ends on 31 December, then as at 31 December 19X5 the balance sheet of the club would include the following items.

(a) *Subscriptions in advance (current liability)*

$90 \text{ members} \times \dfrac{10 \text{ months}}{12 \text{ months}} \times £60 = £4,500$

(b) *Subscriptions in arrears (current asset)*

$$10 \text{ members} \times \frac{2 \text{ months}}{12 \text{ months}} \times £60 = £100$$

It is not uncommon, however, for clubs to take no credit for subscription income until the money is received. In such a case, any subscriptions in arrears are not credited to income and *not* shown as a current asset. It is essential to read the question carefully.

Example: Subscriptions

3.7 At 1 January 19X8, the Little Blithering Debating Society had membership subscriptions paid in advance of £1,600, and subscriptions in arrears of £250. During the year to 31 December 19X8 receipts of subscription payments amounted to £18,400. At 31 December 19X8 subscriptions in advance amounted to £1,750 and subscriptions in arrears to £240.

What is the income from subscriptions to be shown in the income and expenditure account for the year to 31 December 19X8?

Solution: Subscriptions

3.8 The question does not say that subscriptions are only accounted for when received. You may therefore assume that the society takes credit for subscriptions as they become due, whether or not they are received.

The income for the income and expenditure account would be calculated as follows.

		£	£
Payments received in the year			18,400
Add:	subscriptions due but not yet received (ie subscriptions in arrears 31 Dec 19X8)	240	
	subscriptions received last year relating to current year (ie subscriptions in advance 1 Jan 19X8)	1,600	
			1,840
			20,240
Less:	subscriptions received in current year relating to last year (ie subscriptions in arrears 1 Jan 19X8)	250	
	subscriptions received in current year relating to next year (ie subscriptions in advance 31 Dec 19X8)	1,750	
			2,000
Income from subscriptions for the year			18,240

3.9 You may find it simpler to do this calculation as a ledger account.

SUBSCRIPTIONS ACCOUNT

	£		£
Subscriptions in arrears b/f	250	Subscriptions in advance b/f	1,600
I & E a/c (balancing figure)	18,240	Cash	18,400
Subscriptions in advance c/d	1,750	Subscriptions in arrears c/d	240
	20,240		20,240
Subscriptions in arrears b/d	240	Subscriptions in advance b/d	1,750

Bar trading account

3.10 If a club has a bar or cafeteria a separate trading account will be prepared for its trading activities. A bar trading account will contain the following items.

(a) Bar takings

(b) Opening stocks of goods, purchases and closing stocks of goods, to give the cost of bar sales

(c) A gross profit: item (a) minus item (b)

(d) Other expenses directly related to the running of the bar, if any

(e) A net profit: item (c) minus item (d)

The net bar profit is then included under income in the income and expenditure account. A loss on the bar would be included under expenditure.

Life membership

3.11 Some clubs offer membership for life in return for a given lump sum subscription. Life members, having paid this initial lump sum, do not have to pay any further annual subscriptions. In return the club receives a sum of money, which it can then invest, with the annual interest from these investments being accounted for as income in the income and expenditure account.

The 'once-and-for-all' payments from life members are not income relating to the year in which they are received by the club, because the payment is for the life of the members, which can of course be a very long time to come. Because they are long-term payments, they are recorded in the club accounts as an addition to a life membership fund as follows.

DEBIT   Cash
CREDIT   Life membership fund

3.12 The life membership fund is shown in the balance sheet of the club or society immediately after the accumulated fund.

3.13 Life members enjoy the benefits of membership over their life, and so their payment to the club is 'rewarded' as time goes by. Accounting for life membership over time can be explained with an example.

Suppose that Annette Cord pays a life membership fee of £300 to the Tumbledown Tennis Club. The £300 will initially be put into the club's life membership fund. We will suppose that this money is invested by the club, and earns interest of £30 per annum.

3.14 There are two ways of accounting for the life membership fee.

(a) To keep the £300 in the life membership fund until Annette Cord dies. (Since the £300 earns interest of £30 pa this interest can be said to represent income for the club in lieu of an annual subscription.)

When Annette eventually dies (in five years, or 50 years, or whenever) the £300 she contributed can then be transferred (on death of the life member) out of the life membership fund and directly into the accumulated fund.

(b) To write off subscriptions to the life membership fund by transferring a 'fair' amount from the fund into the income and expenditure account. A 'fair' amount will represent the proportion of the total life membership payment which relates to the current year. We do not know how long any life member will live, but if an estimated average life from becoming a life member until death is, say, 20 years, it might seem reasonable to write off payments to the fund over a 20 year period. In each year, one-twentieth of life membership fees would be deducted from the fund and added as income in the income and expenditure account.

In the case of Annette Cord, the annual transfer would be £15, and after 20 years, her contribution to the fund would have been written off in full from the fund and transferred to the income and expenditure accounts of those 20 years.

This transfer of £15 to the income and expenditure account will of course be supplementary to the annual interest of £30 earned by the club each year from investing the fee of £300.

3.15 If method (b) is selected in preference to method (a), the life membership fund could be written down by either a straight line method or a reducing balance method, in much the same way as fixed assets are depreciated - with the exception that it is a capital fund being written off, and the amount of the annual write-off is income to the club, and not an expense like depreciation.

3.16 A further feature of method (b) is that there is no need to record the death of individual members (unlike method (a)). The annual write-off is based on an average expected life of members, and it does not matter when any individual member dies. The same average write off each year will be used.

3.17 A possible reason for preferring method (b) to method (a) is that life membership subscriptions eventually pass through the income and expenditure account as income of the club, which is logically reasonable, since life members although they pay a long time in advance, do eventually enjoy the benefits of membership in return for their payment. Why therefore, should life membership fees be essentially different from ordinary annual membership subscriptions? It is fair that in due course of time, life membership fees should be accounted for as income of the club, to boost the annual surpluses, or reduce the annual deficits.

3.18 In spite of the logical reasons why method (b) should perhaps be preferable, method (a) is still commonly used. In a Central Assessment task, unless you are told about a rate for 'writing off' the life membership fund annually, you should assume that method (a) should be used, where the question gives you information about the death of club life members.

Example: Life membership fund

3.19 The Coxless Rowing Club has a scheme whereby as an alternative to paying annual subscriptions, members can at any time opt to pay a lump sum which gives them membership for life. Lump sum payments received for life membership are held in a life membership fund but then credited to the income and expenditure account in equal instalments over a ten year period, beginning in the year when the lump sum payment is made and life membership is acquired.

The treasurer of the club, Beau Trace, establishes the following information.

(a) At 31 December 19X4, the balance on the life membership fund was £8,250.

(b) Of this opening balance, £1,220 should be credited as income for the year to 31 December 19X5.

(c) During the year to 31 December 19X5, new life members made lump sum payments totalling £1,500.

Task

Show the movements in the life membership fund for the year to 31 December 19X5, and in doing so, calculate how much should be transferred as income from life membership fund to the income and expenditure account.

Solution: Life membership fund

3.20

LIFE MEMBERSHIP FUND

	£	£
As at 31 December 19X4		8,250
New life membership payments received in 19X5		1,500
		9,750
Less transfer to income and expenditure account:		
out of balance as at 31 December 19X4	1,220	
out of new payments in 19X5 (10% of £1,500)	150	
		1,370
Fund as at 31 December 19X5		8,380

The income and expenditure account for the year would show:

Income from life membership	1,370

Accounting for the sale of investments and fixed assets

3.21 In accounting for clubs and societies, the income and expenditure account is used to record the surplus or deficit in the transactions for the year. Occasionally a club or society might sell off some of its investments or fixed assets, and in doing so might make a profit or loss on the sale.

(a) The profit/loss on the sale of an investment is simply the difference between the sale price and the balance sheet value (usually cost) of the investment.

(b) The profit/loss on the sale of a fixed asset is the difference between the sale price and the net book value of the asset at the date of sale.

3.22 There is nothing different or unusual about the accounts of non-trading organisations in computing the amount of such profits or losses. What is different, however, is how the profit or losses should be recorded in the accounts.

(a) The profit or loss on the sale of investments is not shown in the income and expenditure account. Instead, the profit is directly added to (or loss subtracted from) the accumulated fund.

(b) The profit or loss on the sale of a fixed asset which is not subject to depreciation charges in the income and expenditure account, is also taken directly to the accumulated fund.

(c) The profit or loss on the sale of fixed assets which have been subject to depreciation charges is recorded in the income and expenditure account.

3.23 The point of difference in (c) compared with (a) and (b) is that, since depreciation on the asset has been charged in the income and expenditure account in the past, it is appropriate that a profit or loss on sale should also be reported through the account.

Example: Income and expenditure accounts

3.24 The preceding explanations might be sufficient to enable you to prepare an income and expenditure account yourself. A lengthy example is given below and further exercises from the workbook are recommended at the end of the chapter.

3.25 The assets and liabilities of the Berley Sports Club at 31 December 19X4 were as follows.

	£
Pavilion at cost less depreciation	13,098
Bank and cash	1,067
Bar stock	291
Bar debtors	231
Rates prepaid	68
Contributions owing to sports club by users of sports club facilities	778
Bar creditors	427
Loans to sports club	1,080
Accruals: water	13
electricity	130
miscellaneous	75
loan interest	33
Contributions paid in advance by users of sports club facilities	398

A receipts and payments account for the year ended 31 December 19X5 was produced as follows.

	£		£
Opening balance	1,067	Bar purchases	2,937
Bar sales	4,030	Repayment of loan capital	170
Telephone	34	Rent of ground	79
Contributions from users of club		Rates	320
facilities	1,780	Water	38
Socials	177	Electricity	506
Miscellaneous	56	Insurance	221
		Repairs to equipment	326
		Expenses of socials	67
		Maintenance of ground	133
		Wages of groundsman	140
		Telephone	103
		Bar sundries	144
		Loan interest	97
		Miscellaneous	163
		Closing balance	1,700
	7,144		7,144

The following information as at 31 December 19X5 was also provided.

	£
Bar stock	394
Bar debtors	50
Bar creditors	901
Rent prepaid	16
Water charges owing	23
Electricity owing	35
Creditors for bar sundries	65
Contributions by users of sports club facilities:	
owing to sports club	425
paid in advance to sports club	657
Rates prepaid	76

Depreciation on the pavilion for the year was £498.

You are asked to prepare a statement showing the gross and net profits earned by the bar, an income and expenditure account for the year ended 31 December 19X5 and a balance sheet as at that date.

Approach to a solution

3.26 We are not given the size of the accumulated fund as at the beginning of the year, but it can be calculated as the balancing figure to make total liabilities plus capital equal to total assets (as at 31 December 19X4).

Calculation of accumulated fund at 1 January 19X5

	£	£
Assets		
Pavilion at cost less depreciation		13,098
Bank and cash		1,067
Bar stock		291
Bar debtors		231
Rates prepaid		68
Contributions in arrears		778
		15,533
Liabilities		
Bar creditors	427	
Loans	1,080	
Accrued charges £(13 + 130 + 75 + 33)	251	
Contributions received in advance	398	
		2,156
∴ Accumulated fund at 1 January 19X5		13,377

3.27 The next step is to analyse the various items of income and expenditure.

   (a) There is a bar, and so a bar trading account can be prepared.

   (b) Income from the telephone (presumably from members paying the club for calls they make) can be netted off against telephone expenditure.

   (c) The revenue from socials has associated expenses to net off against it.

   (d) There is also miscellaneous income and contributions from club members.

3.28 The bar trading account can only be put together after we have calculated bar sales and purchases.

   (a) We are given bar debtors as at 1 January 19X5 and 31 December 19X5 and also cash received from bar sales. The bar sales for the year can therefore be calculated.

BAR DEBTORS

		£			£
1.1.19X5	Balance b/f	231	31.12.19X5	Cash	4,030
31.12.19X5	∴ Bar sales	3,849	31.12.19X5	Balance c/f	50
		4,080			4,080

   (b) Similarly, purchases for the bar are calculated from opening and closing amounts for bar creditors, and payments for bar purchases.

BAR CREDITORS

		£			£
31.12.19X5	Cash	2,937	1.1.19X5	Balance b/f	427
31.12.19X5	Balance c/f	901	31.12.19X5	∴ Bar purchases	3,411
		3,838			3,838

   (c) Be clear in your own mind that cash receipts from bar sales and cash payments for bar supplies are not the bar sales and cost of bar sales that we want. Cash receipts and payments in the year are not for matching quantities of goods, nor do they relate to the actual goods sold in the year.

   (d) Other bar trading expenses are bar sundries.

	£
Cash payments for bar sundries	144
Add creditors for bar sundries as at 31.12.19X5	65
	209
Less creditors for bar sundries as at 1.1.19X5	0
Expenses for bar sundries for the year	209

3.29 BAR TRADING ACCOUNT
FOR THE YEAR ENDED 31 DECEMBER 19X5

	£	£
Sales		3,849
Cost of sales		
Opening stock	291	
Purchases	3,411	
	3,702	
Less closing stock	394	
		3,308
Gross profit		541
Sundry expenses		209
Net profit		332

3.30 Contributions to the sports club for the year should be calculated in the same way as membership subscriptions. Using a T-account format below, the income from contributions (for the income and expenditure account) is the balancing figure. Contributions in advance brought forward are liabilities (credit balance b/f) and contributions in arrears brought forward are assets (debit balance b/f).

CONTRIBUTIONS

		£			£
1.1.19X5	Balance in arrears b/f	778	1.1.19X5	Balance in advance b/f	398
31.12.19X	∴ Income and expenditure	1,168	31.12.19X5	Cash	1,780
31.12.19X5	Balance in advance c/f	657	31.12.19X5	Balance in arrears c/f	425
		2,603			2,603

3.31 BERLEY SPORTS CLUB INCOME AND EXPENDITURE ACCOUNT
FOR THE YEAR ENDED 31 DECEMBER 19X5

	£	£
Income		
Contributions		1,168
Net income from bar trading		332
Income from socials: receipts	177	
less expenses	67	
		110
Miscellaneous		56
		1,666
Expenses		
Ground rent £(79 – 16)	63	
Rates £(320 + 68 – 76)	312	
Water £(38 – 13 + 23)	48	
Electricity £(506 – 130 + 35)	411	
Insurance	221	
Equipment repairs	326	
Ground maintenance	133	
Wages	140	
Telephone £(103 – 34)	69	
Loan interest £(97 – 33)	64	
Miscellaneous expenses £(163 – 75)	88	
Depreciation	498	
		2,373
Deficit		(707)

BERLEY SPORTS CLUB
BALANCE SHEET AS AT 31 DECEMBER 19X5

	£	£
Fixed assets		
Pavilion at NBV £(13,098 – 498)		12,600
Current assets		
Bar stock	394	
Bar debtors	50	
Contributions in arrears	425	
Prepayments £(16 + 76)	92	
Cash at bank	1,700	
	2,661	
Current liabilities		
Bar creditors £(901 + 65)	966	
Accrued charges	58	
Contributions in advance	657	
	1,681	
Net current assets		980
		13,580
Long-term liability		
Loan £(1,080 – 170)		910
		12,670
Accumulated fund		
Balance at 1 January 19X5		13,377
Less deficit for year		(707)
		12,670

4   MANUFACTURING ACCOUNTS

4.1   A company's trading account will usually include a cost of goods sold derived as the total of opening stock plus purchases, less closing stock. This is particularly suitable for a retail business which buys in goods and sells them on to customers without altering their condition. But for a manufacturing company it would be truer to say that the cost of goods sold is as follows.

	£
Opening stock of finished goods	X
Plus cost of finished goods produced in the period	X
	X
Less closing stock of finished goods	(X)
Cost of finished goods sold	X

4.2   A *manufacturing account* is an account in which the costs of producing finished goods are accumulated. Eventually the 'cost of finished goods produced in the period' is transferred to the trading account as part of the cost of goods sold; this is illustrated above.

4.3   The costs accumulated in a manufacturing account are as follows.

(a)   The cost of raw materials consumed in the period. This is the opening stock of raw materials, plus purchases of raw materials less closing stock of raw materials.

(b)   The cost of direct factory wages. We have seen that the total of (a) and (b) is often referred to as the prime cost.

(c)   Production overheads or factory overheads.

4.4   A pro-forma manufacturing account is set out below with illustrative figures.

MANUFACTURING ACCOUNT
FOR THE YEAR ENDED 31 DECEMBER 19X6

	£	£
Raw materials		
Opening stock	4,000	
Purchases (net of returns)	207,000	
	211,000	
Less closing stock	23,000	
		188,000
Factory wages		21,000
Prime cost		209,000
Production overhead		
Factory power	4,000	
Plant depreciation	3,000	
Plant maintenance	1,500	
Rates and insurance	2,500	
Light and heat	3,000	
Sundry expenses	5,000	
Factory manager's salary	9,000	
Building depreciation	1,000	
		29,000
Production cost of resources consumed		238,000
Work in progress		
Opening stocks	8,000	
Closing stocks	(17,000)	
Increase in work in progress stocks		(9,000)
Factory cost of finished goods produced		229,000

4.5 You may need to think carefully about the adjustment for work in progress near the end of the statement. When a business purchases raw materials they are issued to production departments as required. Employees in the production departments will work on the raw materials in order to convert them eventually into finished goods ready for sale. At the balance sheet date, there will be work in progress in the production departments, ie items which have been partly converted but which have not yet reached the stage of being finished goods.

4.6 The value of this work in progress will include not only the cost of the raw materials, but also the wages of employees who have worked on it plus any attributable overheads. It follows that the prime cost and factory overheads shown in the manufacturing account will not all have resulted in the production of finished goods, because some of the costs may have gone to increase the stocks of work in progress. To arrive at the cost of finished goods produced, any such increase must be deducted from the total costs incurred.

4.7 Of course, if the value of work in progress had *fallen* during the period, this fall would be an *increase* in the cost of finished goods produced.

Example: Manufacturing, trading and profit and loss account

4.8 A manufacturing company has its factory and offices at the same site. Its results for the year to 31 December 19X5 were as follows.

		£
Sales		179,000
Purchases of raw materials		60,000
Direct labour		70,000
Depreciation of equipment		10,000
Local authority rates		5,000
Depreciation of building		2,000
Heating and lighting		3,000
Telephone		2,000
Other manufacturing overheads		2,300
Other administration expenses		2,550
Other selling expenses		1,150

Shared overhead costs are to be apportioned as follows.

	Manufacturing	*Administration*	*Selling*
Depreciation of equipment	80%	5%	15%
Rates	50%	30%	20%
Depreciation of building	50%	30%	20%
Heating and lighting	40%	35%	25%
Telephone	-	40%	60%

The values of stocks are as follows.

	At *1 January 19X5*	*At* *31 December 19X5*
	£	£
Raw materials	5,000	3,000
Work in progress	4,000	3,000
Finished goods	16,000	18,000

Task

Prepare the manufacturing, trading and profit and loss account of the company for the period to 31 December 19X5.

Solution: Manufacturing, trading and profit and loss account

4.9   MANUFACTURING ACCOUNT FOR THE YEAR ENDED 31 DECEMBER 19X5

	£	£
Opening stock of raw materials		5,000
Purchases		60,000
		65,000
Closing stock of raw materials		3,000
Raw materials used in production		62,000
Direct labour		70,000
Prime cost		132,000
Manufacturing overheads		
Depreciation of equipment (80% of £10,000)	8,000	
Rates (50% of £5,000)	2,500	
Depreciation of building (50% of £2,000)	1,000	
Heating and lighting (40% of £3,000)	1,200	
Other expenses	2,300	
		15,000
Manufacturing costs during the year		147,000
Add opening stock of work in progress		4,000
Less closing stock of work in progress		(3,000)
Reduction in stock of work in progress		1,000
Cost of finished goods fully produced,		
transferred to trading account (ie factory cost)		148,000

TRADING AND PROFIT AND LOSS ACCOUNT
FOR THE YEAR ENDED 31 DECEMBER 19X5

	£	£	£
Sales			179,000
Opening stock of finished goods		16,000	
Cost of finished goods produced		148,000	
		164,000	
Closing stock of finished goods		18,000	
Cost of goods sold			146,000
Gross profit			33,000
Selling expenses			
Depreciation of equipment (15% of £10,000)	1,500		
Rates (20% of £5,000)	1,000		
Depreciation of building (20% of £2,000)	400		
Heating and lighting (25% of £3,000)	750		
Telephone (60% of £2,000)	1,200		
Other expenses	1,150		
		6,000	
Administration expenses			
Depreciation of equipment (5% of £10,000)	500		
Rates (30% of £5,000)	1,500		
Depreciation of building (30% of £2,000)	600		
Heating and lighting (35% of £3,000)	1,050		
Telephone (40% of £2,000)	800		
Other expenses	2,550		
		7,000	
			13,000
Net profit			20,000

Transfer prices

4.10 When departments within a business transfer goods to each other during production, it is usually easy to decide which department has incurred which costs relating to those goods. Is it fair, however, to allow only the final department handling the goods to make a profit when they are sold? To be fair to the different parts of the business, each department is often made to 'buy' the goods produced by another department and the price charged may involve an element of profit.

4.11 In manufacturing accounts a 'profit' may be added to the factory cost before it is transferred to the trading and profit and loss account, so that the factory producing the items has an income and a profit. This means that the factory can operate as a 'profit centre', something you will learn about in your later studies of management accounting. The artificial price set by the factory to 'sell' its goods internally is called a 'transfer price'.

4.12 In the above example, if the factory added a 20% profit to its factory cost, then the 'factory profit' would be:

£148,000 × 20% = £29,600

and the transfer price would be £148,000 + £29,600 = £177,600.

4.13 The use of transfer prices means that adjustments would be required in the trading and profit and loss account to give a true net profit. The factory profit would be added to the gross profit on trading and a further adjustment may then be necessary because of unrealised profit included in stock. For example, if stock held at the year end is valued at 'cost' of £21,600, then this includes a factory 'profit' of £21,600 × 20/120 = £3,600 which the business as a whole has not yet earned from an external sale. This adjustment is also required for opening stock, so that there will be a net difference on the unrealised profit adjustment.

4.14 Using the example above, the first part of the trading and profit and loss account would appear as follows.

	£	£
Sales		179,000
Cost of sales		
Opening stock of finished goods (at transfer price)	19,200	
Cost of finished goods produced	177,600	
	196,800	
Closing stock	21,600	
		175,200
		3,800
Factory profit		29,600
		33,400
Change in unrealised profit adjustment		
Opening stock £19,200 × 20/120	3,200	
Closing stock £21,600 × 20/120	3,600	
'True' gross profit, ie as above		(400)
		33,000

Key points in this chapter

- In *club accounts*, the *receipts and payments account* is, in effect, a summary of the cash book. For small clubs with a few straightforward transactions, this statement may be sufficient. For larger concerns, however, the receipts and payments account will form the basis for the preparation of the income and expenditure account and balance sheet.

- *Income and expenditure accounts* are the equivalent of profit and loss accounts for non-trading organisations.

- You should remember to carry out the following when presenting income and expenditure accounts.

  - *Match* the sources of revenue with related costs to show net income from the organisation's various activities.

  - Treat *subscriptions received in advance* as a current liability and (unless the question states the contrary) treat subscriptions in arrears as a current asset.

  - Describe the *result* for the year as surplus or deficit, not as profit or loss.

  - Describe the *capital* of the organisation as the accumulated fund but remember that capital may also include other funds such as a life membership fund.

- *Manufacturing accounts* are prepared for internal management use only. Their purpose is to distinguish between the costs and profitability associated with manufacturing operations and those associated with trading (which are shown in the trading account).

- Manufacturing accounts highlight the following.

  - *Prime cost*: the cost of raw materials and direct labour employed in production.

  - *Factory cost of goods produced*: equal to prime cost plus indirect factory expenses and plus or minus any movement over the period in the cost of work in progress.

  - *Factory profit*: a notional profit earned in manufacturing operations, allowing the factory to 'share' some of the overall profit.

  - *Transfer price of finished goods produced*: equal to factory cost plus factory profit.

For practice on the points covered in this chapter you should now attempt the Practice Exercises in Session 9 of the Financial Accounting Workbook

Part E
Extended trial balance

10 Extended trial balance

This chapter covers the following topics.

1   The extended trial balance and its purpose

2   Preparing the extended trial balance

---

1 THE EXTENDED TRIAL BALANCE AND ITS PURPOSE

1.1 We have already seen what a *trial balance* is: it is a list of all the balances in the ledger accounts, made up before the preparation of the financial statements to check the accuracy of the double entry accounting. The financial statements (the profit and loss account and the balance sheet) are drawn up using the balances in the trial balance.

1.2 Usually this step of drawing up the financial statements from the trial balance involves adjusting a few of the balances in some way. For example:

    (a) correction of errors;
    (b) recognition of accruals and prepayments;
    (c) making provision for depreciation, and bad and doubtful debts; and
    (d) adding in the closing stock figure.

1.3 In order to keep track of such adjustments and set out the necessary figures neatly, an *extended trial balance* may be used.

Format of an extended trial balance

1.4 The extended trial balance gives a vertical list of all the ledger account balances (the trial balance) with four further columns (for adjustments, accruals and prepayments) and then two pairs of further columns which show whether figures go to the profit and loss account or the balance sheet.

1.5 Its columns headings will look something like this:

Ledger account	Trial balance figure		Adjustments		Accruals	Prepayments	Profit and loss a/c		Balance sheet	
	Dr	Cr	Dr	Cr			Dr	Cr	Dr	Cr
	£	£	£	£	£	£	£	£	£	£

1.6 In central assessment questions the proforma given might not include separate columns for accruals and prepayments, in which case they will be treated as adjustments.

2 PREPARING THE EXTENDED TRIAL BALANCE
Centrally assessed 6/94 - 6/97

2.1 The best way to see how the extended trial balance works is to follow through an example.

Example: Extended trial balance

2.2 The ledger accounts of Leigh, a trader, as at 31 December 19X0 before any adjustments have been made to them, are as follows.

	£
Shop fittings at cost	6,000
Depreciation provision at 1 January 19X0	300
Leasehold premises at cost	37,500
Depreciation provision at 1 January 19X0	1,875
Stock in trade at 1 January 19X0	78,000
Debtors at 31 December 19X0	160,500
Provision for doubtful debts at 1 January 19X0	2,880
Cash in hand	150
Cash at bank	12,150
Creditors for supplies	195,000
Proprietor's capital at 1 January 19X0	79,845
Purchases	306,000
Sales	387,000
Wages	54,600
Advertising	6,900
Rates for 15 months to 31 March 19X1	4,500
Bank charges	600

2.3   The adjustments Leigh needs to make to his accounts are:

(a)   depreciation of shop fittings £300;

(b)   depreciation of leasehold £1,875;

(c)   a debt of £1,500 is irrecoverable and is to be written off and the doubtful debts provision is to be increased to 2% of the year end debtors figure;

(d)   the stock in trade at 31 December 19X0 is valued at £90,000;

(e)   on 31 December 19X0, £360 was owed for advertising expenses but an invoice has not yet been received.

2.4   You are required to give effect to these adjustments by using an extended trial balance and to prepare a trading and profit and loss account for the year ended 31 December 19X0 and a balance sheet as at that date.

Solution: Extended trial balance

2.5   The first step is to draw up a trial balance from this list of balances and insert it in the first two columns of the extended trial balance. These are the debit and credit columns, and so first you must sort out the credit balances in the ledger accounts from the debit balances. If there are no errors in the accounts, the total of the debit and credit balances should be equal. The result of this process is shown on Page 166. You should note here that, although in earlier examples we balanced off expense accounts by posting the balance to the trading profit and loss account, in the ETB the opening profit and loss account ledger balance is not adjusted. This is to allow the final profit to be calculated on the ETB, rather than within the profit and loss ledger account.

Part E: Extended trial balance

Folio	Account	Trial balance Debit £	Trial balance Credit £	Adjustments Debit £	Adjustments Credit £	Accrued £	Prepaid £	Profit and loss a/c Debit £	Profit and loss a/c Credit £	Balance sheet Debit £	Balance sheet Credit £
1	Shop fittings	6,000									
2	Shop fittings : dep'n provision		300								
3	Leasehold premises: cost	37,500									
4	Leasehold premises: acc amortisation		1,875								
5	Stock at 1.1.X0	78,000									
6	Sales ledger control account	160,500									
7	Provision for doubtful debts		2,880								
8	Cash in hand	150									
9	Bank	12,150									
10	Purchase ledger control account		195,000								
11	Proprietor's capital at 1.1.X0		79,845								
12	Purchases	306,000									
13	Sales		387,000								
14	Wages	54,600									
15	Advertising	6,900									
16	Rates	4,500									
17	Bank charges	600									
	SUB-TOTAL	666,900	666,900								
	Profit for the year										
	TOTAL	666,900	666,900								

2.6 The next step is to make all the various adjustments. Remember that each adjustment has to be put in twice, in accordance with the rule of double entry (because the extended trial balance, in effect, is like a handy listing of all the ledger accounts). The adjustments fall into three main types.

(a) Accruals and prepayments
(b) Adjustments to stock figure
(c) Other adjustments

2.7 In order to make the explanation easier to follow, it is convenient to look at 'other adjustments' first.

Other adjustments

2.8 Other adjustments will be recorded in the adjustments column in the extended trial balance. In our example, there are five such adjustments.

(a) *Shop fittings depreciation of £300*

DEBIT	Depreciation expense (eventually a deduction in the profit and loss account)
CREDIT	Provision for depreciation: shop fittings

The depreciation expense account does not yet appear in the list of ledger accounts, so we will have to add it on; the credit increases the provision in the balance sheet.

(b) *Leasehold depreciation of £1,875*

DEBIT	Depreciation expense
CREDIT	Provision for depreciation: leasehold

(c) *Write off debt of £1,500*

DEBIT	Bad and doubtful debts (expense)
CREDIT	Sales ledger control a/c

The bad and doubtful debts account does not yet appear in the list of ledger accounts, so we will have to add it on.

(d) *Increase bad debt provision to 2% of debtors*

2% of debtors = 2% of £(160,500 – 1,500)   = £3,180
Increase is therefore £3,180 – £2,880   = £300

DEBIT	Bad and doubtful debts
CREDIT	Provision for doubtful debts

Adjustments to stock figure

2.9 The adjustment required to the stock figure is not quite the same type of adjustment as those described above. You must bring in the closing stocks figure from the stock account, which is drawn up specially for the preparation of financial statements.

2.10 The closing stocks figure of £90,000 is entered into the extended trial balance as follows.

DEBIT	Stock a/c (balance sheet)
CREDIT	Stock a/c (profit and loss account)

So the entries will go into the DR balance sheet column and the CR profit and loss column. Both of these closing stock figures can be given their own ledger accounts and added on to the list of ledger accounts or simply entered in the opening stock account.

Accruals and prepayments

2.11 Advertising expenses of £360 are owed, but have not yet been recorded in the accounts as an invoice has not yet been received. The £360 is an accrued expense, and it is necessary to increase advertising expenses (debit advertising expenses) so that the £360 is debited in the profit and loss account just like any other expenses.

2.12 The 'other side' of the entry is that there should be an accrual of £360 shown in the current liabilities of the balance sheet. We will return to that later. At the moment, the £360 is entered just once, in the accruals column. When we return to it, we will see how it conforms to the rule of double entry.

2.13 There is a prepayment adjustment that has to be made as well. Rates to 31 March 19X0 have been paid, so there is a prepayment of $3/15 \times £4,500 = £900$. The £900 is entered in the prepayments column of the extended trial balance, and the 'other side' of the entry should be a prepayment in the current assets of the balance sheet. In the same way as for accruals, prepayments are entered just once for the time being. We will return to the £900 later.

2.14 The results of entering the adjustments, accruals and prepayments are shown on Page 169.

(a) The total figures for depreciation expenses and bad and doubtful debts expenses have been entered, to make the workings neater.

(b) Every figure has been entered twice except for the accruals and prepayments.

(c) If you had been asked to use a layout which does not have separate accruals and prepayments columns (see Paragraph 1.6) you would debit (for prepayments) or credit (for accruals) an extra prepayments or accruals 'account', added at the bottom of the trial balance.

2.15 Now there is very little left to do.

(a) Add up the accruals figures and the prepayments figures (simple in this case as there is only one of each!) and transfer them to the balance sheet column. Accruals become a liability (a credit entry) in the balance sheet; prepayments are an asset (a debit entry). This completes the double entry for the accruals and prepayments, ie the columns show the 'expense' side of the double entry, so the balance sheet entry of the debtor (prepayment) or creditor (accrual) must still be made.

(b) Add up the other adjustments column, just to make sure that debits equal credits and that you have filled in the adjustments correctly.

(c) Add the figures across the extended trial balance. For example, shop fittings is just £6,000 and will be a balance sheet figure (fixed asset). Provision for depreciation will become £600 (£300 + £300) and is also a balance sheet figure.

(d) Add up the profit and loss debits and credits. The difference between them is the profit (or loss) for the year.

(e) Take the profit (or loss) into the balance sheet and then add up the debits and credits in the balance sheet to make sure that they do, in fact, balance.

The results of these procedures are shown on Page 170.

2.16 We mentioned in Paragraphs 1.6 and 2.14 that the AAT Central Assessment ETB formats do not include separate accruals and prepayment columns. This is nothing to worry about: the accruals and prepayments are entered individually in the adjustments columns in exactly same way. However, the double entry for the expense and the balance sheet entry is completed at the same time by using accounts for accruals and prepayments. This method is not so easy when you have several accruals or prepayments, but the ETB would appear as shown on Page 171 using this method. You can see that the accruals and prepayments account are simply extended into the balance sheet columns.

Folio	Account	Trial balance Debit £	Trial balance Credit £	Adjustments Debit £	Adjustments Credit £	Accrued £	Prepaid £	Profit and loss a/c Debit £	Profit and loss a/c Credit £	Balance sheet Debit £	Balance sheet Credit £
1	Shop fittings	6,000									
2	Shop fittings : dep'n provision		300		300						
3	Leasehold premises: cost	37,500									
4	Leasehold premises: acc amortisation		1,875		1,875						
5	Stock at 1.1.X0	78,000									
6	Sales ledger control account	160,500			1,500						
7	Provision for doubtful debts		2,880		300						
8	Cash in hand	150									
9	Bank	12,150									
10	Purchase ledger control account		195,000								
11	Proprietor's capital at 1.1.X0		79,845								
12	Purchases	306,000									
13	Sales		387,000								
14	Wages	54,600									
15	Advertising	6,900				360					
16	Rates	4,500					900				
17	Bank charges	600									
18	Depreciation expense			2,175							
19	Bad and doubtful debts			1,800							
20	Stock (B/S)			90,000							
21	Stock (P&L)				90,000						
	SUB-TOTAL	666,900	666,900								
	Profit for the year										
	TOTAL	666,900	666,900								

Folio	Account	Trial balance Debit £	Trial balance Credit £	Adjustments Debit £	Adjustments Credit £	Accrued £	Prepaid £	Profit and loss a/c Debit £	Profit and loss a/c Credit £	Balance sheet Debit £	Balance sheet Credit £
1	Shop fittings	6,000								6,000	
2	Shop fittings : dep'n provision		300		300						600
3	Leasehold premises: cost	37,500								37,500	
4	Leasehold premises: acc amortisation		1,875		1,875						3,750
5	Stock at 1.1.X0	78,000						78,000			
6	Sales ledger control account	160,500			1,500					159,000	
7	Provision for doubtful debts		2,880		300						3,180
8	Cash in hand	150								150	
9	Bank	12,150								12,150	
10	Purchase ledger control account		195,000								195,000
11	Proprietor's capital at 1.1.X0		79,845								79,845
12	Purchases	306,000						306,000			
13	Sales		387,000						387,000		
14	Wages	54,600						54,600			
15	Advertising	6,900				360		7,260			
16	Rates	4,500					900	3,600			
17	Bank charges	600						600			
18	Depreciation expense			2,175				2,175			
19	Bad and doubtful debts			1,800				1,800			
20	Stock (B/S)			90,000						90,000	
21	Stock (P&L)				90,000				90,000		
	Prepayments/accruals					360	900			900	360
	SUB-TOTAL	666,900	666,900	93,975	93,975	360	900	454,035	477,000	305,700	282,735
	Profit for the year							22,965			22,965
	TOTAL	666,900	666,900	93,975	93,975	360	900	477,000	477,000	305,700	305,700

Account	Trial balance Debit £	Trial balance Credit £	Adjustments Debit £	Adjustments Credit £	Profit and loss a/c Debit £	Profit and loss a/c Credit £	Balance sheet Debit £	Balance sheet Credit £
Shop fittings	6,000						6,000	
Shop fittings : dep'n provision		300		300				600
Leasehold premises: cost	37,500						37,500	
Leasehold premises: acc amortisation		1,875		1,875				3,750
Stock at 1.1.X0	78,000				78,000			
Sales ledger control account	160,500			1,500			159,000	
Provision for doubtful debts		2,880		300				3,180
Cash in hand	150						150	
Bank	12,150						12,150	
Purchase ledger control account		195,000						195,000
Proprietor's capital at 1.1.X0		79,845						79,845
Purchases	306,000				306,000			
Sales		387,000				387,000		
Wages	54,600				54,600			
Advertising	6,900		360		7,260			
Rates	4,500			900	3,600			
Bank charges	600				600			
Depreciation expense			2,175		2,175			
Bad and doubtful debts			1,800		1,800			
Stock (B/S)			90,000				90,000	
Stock (P&L)				90,000		90,000		
Accruals				360				360
Prepayments			900				900	
SUB-TOTAL	666,900	666,900	95,235	95,235	454,035	477,000	305,700	282,735
Profit for the year					22,965			22,965
TOTAL	666,900	666,900	95,235	95,235	477,000	477,000	305,700	305,700

2.17   Although Unit 5 does not require the preparation of the balance sheet or profit and loss account from the ETB, it will be useful if you can see how the finished product is derived. The final step is to use the figures in the last two columns of the extended trial balance to draw up the balance sheet and profit and loss account. For this example, the result would be as follows.

LEIGH
TRADING AND PROFIT AND LOSS ACCOUNT
FOR THE YEAR ENDED 31 DECEMBER 19X0

	£	£
Sales		387,000
Less cost of sales	78,000	
Purchases	306,000	
	384,000	
Less closing stock	90,000	
		294,000
Gross profit		93,000
Less expenses		
Wages	54,600	
Advertising	7,260	
Rates	3,600	
Bank charges	600	
Depreciation: fixtures	300	
fittings	1,875	
Bad debt written off	1,500	
Increase in provision for doubtful debts	300	
		70,035
Net profit		22,965

LEIGH
BALANCE SHEET AS AT 31 DECEMBER 19X0

	Cost £	Dep'n £	NBV £
Fixed assets			
Leasehold	37,500	3,750	33,750
Fixtures	6,000	600	5,400
	43,500	4,350	39,150
Current assets			
Stock		90,000	
Debtors	159,000		
Less provision for bad and doubtful debts	3,180		
		155,820	
Prepayments		900	
Cash at bank		12,150	
Cash in hand		150	
		259,020	
Current liabilities			
Trade creditors		195,000	
Accruals		360	
		195,360	
Net current assets			63,660
			102,810
Capital			
At 1 January 19X0			79,845
Profit for year			22,965
At 31 December 19X0			102,810

Computerising the extended trial balance

2.18   Like other accounting activities, the extended trial balance can be computerised. The AAT has stated that students should develop competence in both manual and computer processing methods in Units 4, 5 and 6.

(a)   The computer could be programmed to do all the work itself. The trial balance would be input (or the computer might already have drawn it up from the ledger accounts) and then the individual corrections would be input. The computer would go ahead and produce the financial statements by itself.

(b) The extended trial balance could be prepared using a spreadsheet package. That is, it would look just like the example in this chapter, but it would be on a screen instead of paper. It would be used just as a handwritten version would be used, except that numbers would be keyed in rather than written down. In this sort of 'computerised' extended trial balance, the computer would do some of the arithmetic, but the human operator would still be doing a lot of the work. A large number of spreadsheet exercises involving extended trial balances may be found in the Units 21 and 22 *Information Technology* Combined Text.

The extended trial balance and the journal

2.19 Normally, when an error is found, it is entered into the journal and then the correcting entries are made in the relevant ledger accounts. So in an ideal world, when the trial balance and the extended trial balance are drawn up, corrections of errors have already been incorporated into the ledger account balances.

2.20 In practice, some errors are not discovered until the last minute (for example, perhaps the auditor of the accounts, who often carry out their work at year-end, discover some errors). When this happens, the corrections are entered in the journal, and their effect must be noted on the extended trial balance, in the 'other adjustments' column.

The importance of practice

2.21 Extended trial balance exercises are likely to occur both in central and devolved assessments. They will also form a substantial part of your central assessment for Unit 14 of the Technician stage. The principles are logical and straightforward, but you will not be able to master the technique with sufficient accuracy and speed without a great deal of practice. A considerable amount of practice material is provided in the accompanying *Financial Accounting* Workbook.

Key points in this chapter

- An *extended trial balance* is used to adjust trial balance figures for:
  o errors;
  o accruals and prepayments;
  o provisions (depreciation, bad and doubtful debts);
  o closing stock figures.
- The extended trial balance is basically a *worksheet* representing all the ledger account balances and what happens to them.
- The ETB produces *balances* which can be taken directly to the balance sheet and profit and loss account.
- Since the ETB will be an important feature of your Unit 4 and 5 assessments it is important to *practise* ETB tasks as much as possible, both manually and on a spreadsheet.

For practice on the points covered in this chapter you should now attempt the Practice Exercises in Session 10 of the Financial Accounting Workbook

Index

ORDER FORM

Any books from our AAT range can be ordered by telephoning 0181-740 2211. Alternatively, send this page to our Freepost address or fax it to us on 0181-740 1184.

To: BPP Publishing Ltd, FREEPOST, London W12 8BR　　　**Tel: 0181-740 2211**
　　　　　　　　　　　　　　　　　　　　　　　　　　　　　　Fax: 0181-740 1184

Forenames (Mr / Ms): _____

Surname: _____

Address: _____

_____

Post code: _____

Please send me the following books:

		Price Interactive Text	Kit	Quantity Interactive Text	Kit	Total
		£	£			£
Foundation						
Unit 1	Cash Transactions	9.95		....		....
Unit 2	Credit Transactions	9.95		....		....
Unit 1 & 2	Cash & Credit Transactions Devolved Ass'mt		9.95		....	....
Unit 1 & 2	Cash & Credit Transactions Central Ass'mt		9.95		....	....
Unit 3	Payroll Transactions (9/97)	9.95		....		....
Unit 3	Payroll Transactions Devolved Ass'mt (9/97)		9.95		....	....
Unit 20	Data Processing (DOS) (7/95)	9.95*		....		....
Unit 20	Data Processing (Windows)	9.95		....		....
Units 24-28	Business Knowledge	9.95		....		....

		Tutorial Text	Workbook	Tutorial Text	Workbook	
Intermediate						
Units 4&5	Financial Accounting	10.95	10.95	....	....	....
Unit 6	Cost Information	10.95	10.95	....	....	....
Units 7&8	Report and Returns	10.95	10.95	....	....	....
Units 21&22	Information Technology	10.95*		....		....
Technician						
Unit 9	Cash Management & Credit Control	10.95	8.95	....	....	....
Unit 10	Managing Accounting Systems	10.95	6.95	....	....	....
Units 11,12&13	Management Accounting	16.95	10.95	....	....	....
Unit 14	Financial Statements	10.95	8.95	....	....	....
Unit 18	Auditing	10.95	6.95	....	....	....
Unit 19	Taxation (FA 97) (10/97)	10.95	8.95	....	....	....
Unit 23	Information Management Systems	10.95	6.95	....	....	....
Units 10,18&23	Project Guidance		6.95		....	....
Unit 25	Health and Safety at Work	3.95**		....		....

* Combined Text

**Price includes postage; this booklet is an extract from Units 24-28 Business Knowledge (Interactive Text)

Postage & packaging:

UK: £2.00 for first plus £2.00 for each extra book.　　　　　　　......... ....

Europe (inc ROI): £4.00 for first plus £2.00 for each extra book.　......... ....

Rest of the World: £6.00 for first plus £4.00 for each extra book.　......... .... _____

　　　　　　　　　　　　　　　　　　　　　　　　　　　　　Total　‾‾‾‾‾‾‾‾‾

I enclose a cheque for £ _____ or charge to Access/Visa/Switch

Card number ☐☐☐☐☐☐☐☐☐☐☐☐☐☐☐☐☐☐☐

Start date (Switch only) _____　**Expiry date** _____　**Issue no. (Switch only)** _____

Signature _____

REVIEW FORM & FREE PRIZE DRAW

All original review forms from the entire BPP range, completed with genuine comments, will be entered into one of two draws on 31 January 1998 and 31 July 1998. The names on the first four forms picked out on each occasion will be sent a cheque for £50.

Name: _____   Address: _____

_____

_____

How have you used this Tutorial Text?
(Tick one box only)

☐ Home study (book only)

☐ On a course: college _____

☐ With 'correspondence' package

☐ Other _____

Why did you decide to purchase this Tutorial Text? *(Tick one box only)*

☐ Have used complementary Workbook

☐ Have used BPP Texts in the past

☐ Recommendation by friend/colleague

☐ Recommendation by a lecturer at college

☐ Saw advertising

☐ Other _____

During the past six months do you recall seeing/receiving any of the following?
(Tick as many boxes as are relevant)

☐ Our advertisement in *Accounting Technician* Magazine

☐ Our advertisement in *PASS*

☐ Our brochure with a letter through the post

Which (if any) aspects of our advertising do you find useful?
(Tick as many boxes as are relevant)

☐ Prices and publication dates of new editions

☐ Information on Tutorial Text content

☐ Facility to order books off-the-page

☐ None of the above

Have you used the companion Workbook for this subject?   ☐ Yes   ☐ No

Your ratings, comments and suggestions would be appreciated on the following areas

	Very useful	Useful	Not useful
Introductory section (How to use this Tutorial Text, etc)	☐	☐	☐
Coverage of elements of competence	☐	☐	☐
Examples	☐	☐	☐
Exercises	☐	☐	☐
Index	☐	☐	☐
Structure and presentation	☐	☐	☐

	Excellent	Good	Adequate	Poor
Overall opinion of this Tutorial Text	☐	☐	☐	☐

Do you intend to continue using BPP Tutorial Texts/Workbooks?   ☐ Yes   ☐ No

Please note any further comments and suggestions/errors on the reverse of this page

Please return to: Neil Biddlecombe, BPP Publishing Ltd, FREEPOST, London, W12 8BR

REVIEW FORM & FREE PRIZE DRAW (continued)

Please note any further comments and suggestions/errors below

FREE PRIZE DRAW RULES

1 Closing date for 31 January 1998 draw is 31 December 1997. Closing date for 31 July 1998 draw is 30 June 1998.

2 Restricted to entries with UK and Eire addresses only. BPP employees, their families and business associates are excluded.

3 No purchase necessary. Entry forms are available upon request from BPP Publishing. No more than one entry per title, per person. Draw restricted to persons aged 16 and over.

4 Winners will be notified by post and receive their cheques not later than 6 weeks after the relevant draw date. Lists of winners will be published in BPP's *focus* newsletter following the relevant draw.

5 The decision of the promoter in all matters is final and binding. No correspondence will be entered into.